# The Breastplate
# of the
# High Priest

*Unlocking the Mystery of the Living Stones*

## Gwen Mouliert

**KP**
KeeperPublishing

THE BREASTPLATE OF THE HIGH PRIEST

Cover design by KeeperGraphics CS, www.keepergraphics.com

Grunge© Javarman | Dreamstime.com

Antique Key© Connie Larsen | Dreamstime.com

KeeperPublishing and KeeperGraphics are a part of Gervaro Enterprises, LLC., located in northern New Jersey.

Published by: KeeperPublishing
Gervaro Enterprises, LLC
PO Box 175,
Swartswood, NJ 07877
rgervasi@keepergraphics.com

Printed in the United States of America.

# Acknowledgement

Primarily, I would like to give glory to God and the Holy Spirit for the awesome truths that He revealed to me concerning the stones of beauty.

I would like to thank the Body of Christ, for their prayerful and financial support during the writing of this book.

Finally, to my husband and family whom I love and thank for your continued encouragement and support.

# $\mathcal{P}$reface

1 Peter 2:9 *"But ye are a chosen generation, a royal priesthood, a holy nation, a peculiar people; that ye should show forth the praises of him who hath called you out of darkness into his marvelous light."*

Not only are we a priesthood but we are living stones, *"Ye also, as lively stones, are built up a spiritual house, a holy priesthood, to offer up spiritual sacrifices, acceptable to God by Jesus Christ."* 1 Peter 2:5

So let us find out about the stones that covered the heart of the priest. Peter tells us that we are living stones and a royal priesthood to show forth the glory of God. Since Jesus is our High Priest, we are the stones on his heart. If you are not familiar with the breastplate of the High Priest, we will look at the stones set over his heart.

This teaching will help you to arise, shine, and walk in the calling that God has placed on your life. We are kings and priests before our God. May each of us wear the stones of beauty to reflect His light.

Blessings in Jesus name,

Gwen Mouliert

# Table of Contents

# *Introduction*

Many years ago the Lord spoke to me while I was reading the book of Ezekiel. He had me stop at a phrase in chapter 28 of Ezekiel. In this chapter, before Satan fell, and before he became the devil, his name was Lucifer. It said he had a *"covering of beautiful stones"* and that *"he walked up and down in the presence of God, in the midst of these beautiful stones."* After reading this the Lord said, *"Look at the verse,"* so I meditated upon the verse. I discovered that *Lucifer* means, "morning star" and "son of the morning." This refers to the time before his rebellion against God, when he was in the Garden of Eden with God and the stones were his covering. He had nine stones. Now the high priest wore what they call an ephod or breastplate. The breastplate had twelve stones in it. Several years back the Lord said to me "Why is it that Satan has nine stones out of the twelve stones? What was the significance of the missing row of stones?" I have to tell you that I have had this revelation in my heart on this for many years now and I am so glad to be able to write about it. The Holy Spirit caused me to pursue this study with a passion. The more I searched the Scripture, I began to realize that I had not heard of anyone else writing on this revelation. I don't know of anyone who has noticed the connection between the nine stones of Lucifer and the twelve stones of the high priest.

I will begin with an overview of the Twelve Tribes of Israel in chapter one. Then in each chapter thereafter, I will go over one stone of the breastplate per chapter. I will also go over the blessings of Jacob and Moses, which were spoken over the Twelve Tribes.

It is important to remind you that Hebrew is written and read from right to left, rather than left to right. When reading this book, and observing the stones, an English-speaking person of the Western world would think the first stone is a carbuncle of Zebulun. It is not; the carbuncle of Zebulun is the third stone. Because the original Hebrew is read from, right to left, this would make the first stone in the breastplate is the Sardius of Judah.

In preparation for impartation, each chapter begins with an opening prayer. Also, please take notice of the Key Definitions throughout this book. You will be enriched and receive profound understanding as these definitions are included in the revelatory Key Points and Closing Prayer at the end of each chapter.

# CHAPTER 1

# The Twelve Tribes of Israel

*Father, I thank you for the Word of God. I thank you that the Bible says heaven and earth will pass away but your Word remains forever. Thank you that even in the book of Psalms it says, "You have magnified your Word even above your name." Lord, I am asking that you would indeed magnify your Word to us and that there would be impartation for understanding so that hearts and minds will be opened upon reading this book. I pray that realization of 1st Peter, chapter 2 would come alive and that because of Christ we would become living stones. Lord Jesus, cause each of us to know the significance of each one of the stones on the breastplate of the high priest. Thank you that Jesus is our High Priest and that He carries us like living stones over His heart into the presence of His Father. In Jesus name, I pray. Amen.*

In order to begin I must give you a brief overview of the linage of Jacob, the father of the twelve tribes that we will be studying. Let us start in Genesis chapters 27-29 where we meet a man named Jacob who deceives his dying father. He put on his brother's clothes and acted like he was his brother Esau and he robbed his brother of his blessing. When his father and brother found out what he had done, he had to flee for his life. Later in verses 43 and 44 of chapter 27, Rebekah, Jacobs mother, says *"Now therefore, my son, obey my voice; arise, flee thou to Laban my brother to Haran; and tarry with him a few days, until thy brother's fury turn away."*

In Genesis chapters 28 & 29, we see Jacob fleeing from Beersheba to Haran where he sees Rachel tending sheep at the well. As soon as he sees her beauty, Jacob kisses Rachel and weeps. He falls in love. He goes back to meet Laban and asks for Rachel's hand in marriage. Laban agrees to give his daughter to Jacob but he requires that Jacob work seven year for her. Jacob worked seven years *"and they seemed unto him but a few days, for the love he had for her."* Laban ends up deceiving him by giving his eldest daughter Leah. Now, I use to be very baffled by this. What kind of man can spend the whole night with someone and not realize until the morning, that he was with the wrong woman?

In biblical times, the marriage was official at the time of engagement. There was no religious rite that was performed with the concluding of the marriage, although there was a feast at the conclusion of the festivities. An engaged woman was, in the eyes of the people, legally married. When the marriage itself was consummated, the husband received the wife and the family of the wife received a dowry. This payment was made because; as the wife's family had given their flesh and blood, the husband's family was bound to give in order to maintain balance between the families. The payment of the (Mohar or dowry) was simply compensation for the loss of the daughter's labor and was not to be considered as a wedding gift.

Imagine what Jacob must have thought, as everything was veiled except her eyes, it was very dark in the tent; because in the morning, once the sun came up, Jacob must have cried out, Oh, no! I do not love you, Leah! I love your sister, Rachel! How many of you know that Jacob deceived his father and now his father-in-law had deceived him. It might take sometime, but what goes around, comes around. Even after all that, Jacob loved Rachel so much that he agreed to work another seven years in order marry her.

The Key Definition for *Jacob* means "a trickster or a deceiver." That is why when Jacob encountered God; they wrestled and struggled, leaving Jacob to say to God, *"I will not let you go until you bless me."* The way God blessed Jacob was by changing his name from Jacob, trickster and deceiver to Israel, "a prince with God" or "one who prevails with God." Can you get excited about the fact that our nature has been changed, and that we are not who we once were before we met Christ.

The Key Definition for *Rachel* is "a ewe meaning a female sheep." The Key Definition for *Leah* means "Weary, to be out of strength." Laban did not want to break the customs, and traditions of his time, which required the eldest daughter to be given in marriage before any of the young siblings. Therefore, he gave Jacob his first born daughter Leah.

> Genesis 29 verse 24-30. *"And Laban gave unto his daughter Leah Zilpah his maid for an handmaid. And it came to pass, that in the morning, behold, it was Leah: and he said to Laban, What is this thou hast done unto me? Did not I serve with thee for Rachel? Wherefore then, hast thou beguiled me? And Laban said, it must not be so done in our country, to give the younger before the firstborn. Fulfill her week, and we will give thee this also for the service which thou shalt serve with me yet seven years. And Jacob did so, and fulfilled her week: and he gave him Rachel his daughter to wife also. And Laban gave to Rachel his daughter Bilhah his handmaid to be her maid. And he went in also unto Rachel, and he loved Rachel more than Leah, and served with him yet seven other years."*

The Key Definition for Rachel's handmaiden *Bilhah* means "to be troubled, to be anxious and upset." The Key Definition for Leah's handmaiden *Zilpah* is "trickling, a very slow flowing river."

Just as Leah and Rachel were opposite in their personalities, so were these two handmaidens. One is anxious, troubled, and upset; while the other handmaiden just goes with the flow.

> Genesis 29:31-32 *"And when the LORD saw that Leah was hated, heopened her womb: but Rachel was barren. And Leah conceived, and bare a son, and she called his name Reuben: for she said, Surely the LORD hath looked upon my affliction; now therefore my husband will love me."*

I believe this is one of the saddest Scriptures in the Bible describing awoman's heart. Leah knows Jacob does not love her and that he wants to be with her sister. It actually says in verse 31 *"that she was hated."* For helongest time I was not sure who hated her, was it Rachel? Notice all sorts of jealousy coming from Rachel in Chapter 30. Was Rachel jealous because Leah had Jacob first on that wedding night, or was it Jacob her husbandwho hated Leah?

Therefore, when looking at Genesis chapter 29 verse 31 you may not really sure who hated Leah. I think in verse 32 it makes it clear that it was her husband, Jacob. It says that when the Lord saw she was hated, it was as if He said: 'I will do something for you; I will open your womb and let you conceive a child.' During biblical times, barrenness was considered a curse. In addition, the birth of a female child was often deemed less significant. A girl was viewed as 'second best' compared to the birth of a son. The function of a woman in biblical times was to produce a son for her husband so that the family name and heritage would continue. If you did not have a son, you kept trying to have one.

So what does God do for Leah, this weary woman? He gives her a son and she names her first-born son Reuben. Reuben is the first-born son to Jacob, the father of the Twelve Tribes. The Key Definition for *Reuben* is, "behold a firstborn son."

Sure enough in verse 32, Leah must think, now he will love me. I am not in an unhappy marriage, but for those women who are, I often remind them that God feels your pain. God is very aware of everything. It says the 'Lord saw that she was afflicted; the Lord saw that she was hated and the Lord gave her a male child.' Verse 33: *"And she conceived again, and bare a son; and said, Because the LORD hath heard I was hated, he hath therefore given me this son also: and she called his name Simeon."*

The Key Definition for *Simeon* is "God heard me in my affliction" or "God heard my cry." Not to offend anyone, but if Jacob hates her so much, how could the two of them have remained so active? I mean, if you hate me then why are you sleeping with me? The story continues and they conceive yet another son. Verse 34: *"And she conceived again, and bare a son; and said, Now this time will my husband be joined unto me, because I have born him three sons: therefore was his name called Levi."*

In verse 34 I would venture to say, she is thinking; 'well, he still does not love me, even though I have given him three sons.' *Reuben,* behold a first born son and *Simeon,* God heard me in my affliction. The Key Definition for *Levi* means to "be joined together." She even states this in the verse, *"maybe now my husband will be joined to me."*

Verse 35 continues, *"And she conceived again, and bare a son: and she said,*

*Now will I praise the LORD: therefore she called his name Judah; and left bearing."* Do you understand that we are condensing five years in four verses. Pregnancy still took nine months back then, the same as now. Therefore, it takes at least four years to get from verse 34-35. Now she is pregnant again.

The Key Definition for *Judah* is "praise be unto God." Maybe she was thinking, 'my husband hates me, he doesn't want to be joined to me. I am only a sexual object to him. He just takes me when he wants me. I have gone through four painful, childbearing experiences.' The minute Leah got her eyes off of her pain about her husband who didn't love her a new chapter started for her.

Notice that everything in her life changes when she names this baby *Judah.* In verse 35, at the end of this chapter, she gets her mind off her sister, she forgets about her pain, allowing her to take her mind off her disappointment. She makes a decision; that no matter what the circumstance or situation is, I am going to praise the Lord!

The moment she changes her focus and names her son *Judah,* "praise be unto God," everything changes.

Let us review the four Key Definitions:

1. Behold a son
2. God heard me in my affliction
3. Be joined together
4. Praise be unto God

We need to move back and check on Rachel, in Genesis chapter 30 verse 1 *"And when Rachel saw that she bare Jacob no children, Rachel envied her sister; and said unto Jacob, Give me children, or else I die."* One of the first things we have seen written about Rachel, except for the fact that she was beautiful, and as lovely as a ewe lamb, is that she 'envied her sister.'

This is a whole other teaching for women on; 'it isn't all about your looks.' Believe me, we have all seen some beautiful women on the exterior and yet they are uglier than sin on the inside; I have met some unattractive in appearance that are beautiful on the inside; because of their character and their nature.

Now Rachel, the one who was beautiful, loved, appreciated, and younger, is miserable. Consumed with envy as her sister Leah has given her husband Jacob four sons. Rachel had been sleeping with the exact same man as her sister for the same number of years, yet she was still childless.

Genesis 30:2: *"And Jacob's anger was kindled against Rachel: and he said,am I in God's stead, who hath withheld from thee the fruit of the womb?"*

Jacob knows that God closed Rachel's womb. Do you know why Jacob is angry? He does not know how to tell her, 'Honey, I am not the one with the problem. You have the problem, because Leah and I are not having any problems. We are doing just fine; we have had four sons in five years. Therefore, Rachel, I do not know how to tell you this, but it is you!'

Genesis 30:3: *"And she said, Behold my maid Bilhah, go in unto her; and she shall bear upon my knees, that I may also have children by her."*

Here we go: 'Okay Jacob, you are married to Leah, and also to me and now I want you to impregnate my handmaiden. As soon as she has a baby, that will be my son.' Genesis chapter 30 verses 4-5: *"And she gave him Bilhah her handmaid to wife: and Jacob went in unto her. And Bilhah conceived, and bare Jacob a son."*

Now he has three wives. He was quite the man at sowing his seed, wasn't he? Remember, the last thing we heard from Leah (who was hated, afflicted, and unloved) was "I'm going to praise God."

In verse 6, listen to what Rachel had to say, "God hath judged me, and hath also heard my voice, and hath given me a son: therefore she called his name Dan." The only thing she cared about was judging. She had judged herself less than a good woman and judged her sister to be a better woman than she was. Leaving her every thought to, 'I'm going to make sure that this gets judged.' Due to what Rachel believed was a judgment from God she now has a surrogate son; "Dan" belongs to her husband but was born to Bilhah.

The Key Definition for *Dan* is "judge, or to pass a judgment." Therefore, Rachel must be thinking, 'okay sister, you think you're having all of these sons? I'll get a son somehow.' Verse 7: *"And Bilhah Rachel's maid conceived again, and bare Jacob a second son."*

Remember, Rachel is not the one who is having these children, it is her handmaiden Bilhah. Verse 8: *"And Rachel said, with great wrestlings have I wrestled with my sister, and I have prevailed: and she called his name Naphtali."*

I do not know about you, but I can see that all is not well with Rachel. I would rather be a Leah than a Rachel. Even though Rachel had everything on the surface, she really did not have the things that were valuable in life. She wants judgment to be passed on Leah. In verse 8, instead of being overwhelmed with joy, 'she wrestled and felt as if she prevailed against her sister.'

Rachel named her second surrogate son Naphtali. The Key Definition of *Naphtali* is "to struggle" and "to wrestle." Those are the only two sons that are born by Bilhah.

Let us get back to Leah. Verses 9-11: *"When Leah saw that she had left bearing, she took Zilpah her maid, and gave her Jacob to wife. Moreover, Zilpah, Leah's handmaiden, bare Jacob a son. And Leah said, A troop cometh: and she called his name Gad."*

Leah also accomplished having a surrogate son and named him Gad. The Key Definition for *Gad* is "fortunate." Remember, that this scripture is talking about Leah! The minute she put her eyes on the Lord and said, 'Judah, Yahweh, I praise you. You are my light and my strength. I am so glad and fortunate. Even though this baby did not come out of my womb, I'm fortunate.' However, on the contrary, Leah's sister Rachel who has been barren and has had babies through her handmaiden is saying, 'I judged you. In addition, I wrestled and struggled with you. You bet I will prevail.'

Meanwhile, in verses 12-13 Zilpah who is Leah's handmaiden bore Jacob a second son, and Leah said, *"Happy am I, for the daughters will call me blessed,"* naming this son *Asher*.

The Key Definition for *Asher* is "to be blessed and happy." Something happened in the heart of Leah. Even though this chapter is on the tribes, I hope you understand that no matter what is coming in your life, that if you could somehow send Judah first. If you could somehow say, 'I will praise the Lord no matter what.' If you could praise Him with tears running down your face and declare, 'He is my praise and I don't care what I have to go through.' Your attitude, heart, and life can change and will change as His word states.

Here is her bitter and jealous sister saying, 'I wrestled, I prevailed and I will beat you sister!' Moreover, in the midst of all this Leah is saying, 'I am just so fortunate because God has blessed me.' You do not hear Leah talk about her husband Jacob anymore. You do not hear her say that she wants him to love her. Her love is now focused on the Lord.

Let us review. We see the two sons born to Zilpah are named *Gad,* which means to be fortunate, and *Asher,* which is to be blessed and happy. After all these years as we read on, you will see that Leah is going to get pregnant again. At this point approximately eight years have passed and Rachel remains barren.

Continuing in Genesis 30 verse 17: *"And God hearkened unto Leah, and she conceived, and bare Jacob the fifth son."* Understand that Jacob has more than five sons; however, this is the fifth son with Leah. Verse 18: *"And Leah said, God hath given me my hire, because I have given my maiden to my husband: and she called his name Issachar."*

The Key Definition for *Issachar* is "to be rewarded." Therefore, Leah sent from being afflicted, and hated, to being blessed, happy, and rewarded. How many of us know that it is all about attitude. You can call it what you want, but it has to remain internal, and it is all about how we perceive things that come against our lives. Verses 19-21: *"And Leah conceived gain, and bare Jacob the sixth son. And Leah said God hath endued me with a good dowry; now will my husband dwell with me, because I have born him six sons: and she called his name Zebulun. Afterwards she bares a daughter, and called her name Dinah."*

The Key Definition for *Zebulun* is "to dwell with honor." I do not know if you recall the scripture 1 Peter chapter 3 verse 7 where it talks about 'husbands, dwell with your wives according to knowledge, giving honor to the weaker vessel.' Let me show you something that is a little off the track, but it is very important to the mission.

Leah was trying to accomplish three things from her husband and these three things will enhance any marriage. I have been married 40 years plus and I think I can tell you the three things a woman wants and the bible backs me up.

The three things a woman wants:

1. To be loved by her husband. (Genesis 29:31-32)
2. For her husband to be joined to her. (Genesis 29:34)
3. For her husband to dwell with her. (Genesis 30:20)

So far, we have learned about ten of the sons born to Jacob. Therefore, we are missing the last two, because there were twelve sons born to Jacob.

Genesis 30:22-24: *"And God remembered Rachel and God hearkened to her, and opened her womb. And she conceived, and bare a son; and said, God hath taken away my reproach: And she called his name Joseph; and said, The LORD shall add to me another son."*

Rachel says in this verse 23 that *"God has taken away my reproach."* that is wrong with this woman? The only thing she cares about is getting even with her sister. She is making sure that she gets to judge as she continues to wrestle and prevail. Finally, after her husband has been with three other women, and has ten sons, let us look at the first thing she thinks about.

The first thing she thinks of, after having Joseph is that her reproach will be taken away. In the Jewish culture of her time, this may have been an appropriate response of grateful relief on her part, that her shame and reproach, was taken away by God through the birth of a son. In verse 24, we see that Rachel called her first son Joseph and 'declares that the Lord would add to her another son.' The Key Definition for *Joseph* is "to add on" or "add to." It is evident that the Bible states, 'Jacob favored Joseph.' Jacob waited ten long years to have a son with the woman he loved from the very beginning.

I don't know how many years, but quite a bit of time has passed, as we begin to read:

Genesis 35:16-20: *"And they journeyed from Bethel ; and there was but a little way to come to Ephrath: and Rachel travailed, and she had hard labor. And it came to pass, when she was in hard labor, that the midwife said unto her, Fear not; thou shalt have this son also. And it came to pass, as her soul was in departing, (for she died) that she called his name Benoni: but his father called him Benjamin. And Rachel died, and was buried in the way to Ephrath, which is Bethlehem . In addition, Jacob set a pillar upon her grave: that is the pillar of Rachel's grave unto this day."*

Here is a woman who dies in childbirth. I personally do not believe that you can live a long life if you are angry, bitter, and resentful. As Rachel is dying, she names her son *Benoni.* The Key definition for *Benoni* is "son of my sorrows." That is the last thing we have recorded in regards to Rachel. This beautiful shepherdess, who was favored by her father, was an attractive woman, and loved by her husband Jacob; ends up dying and with her last breath calls her new born son; *"you are the son of all my sorrows."*

In essence, Jacob said, 'I am not going to have this child be reminded of the sorrow of his mother and my wife dying.' This was not his fault, so Jacob changed his name to Benjamin. The Key definition for *Benjamin* means "son of my right hand or the son at my right hand." We all have a Savior, He is called, "a Man of Sorrow" who also became the Son seated at the right hand of God the Father.

Joseph left his homeland at 17 years old because several brothers had the same envious and jealous spirit their mother Rachel had. The brothers end up selling Joseph into slavery. I am sure you remember the story.

Joseph was 30 years old when he was released from prison and for seven years, there was plenty in the land of Egypt. Then a famine hit and it was during this event that Joseph was reunited with his father. Jacob lived 17 years in Egypt with Joseph and all of his family. Joseph forgave his brothers.

Let's see what happens when Jacob dies. Many times through the bible, people knew when they were going to die. They would gather all the children to include the children's children, at which point they would lay hands on them and bless them. Jacob is an old man and is about to die, so the family was gathered.

Even Peter said, in 2 Peter chapter 1 verse 14, *"Knowing that shortly I must put off this my tabernacle, even as our Lord Jesus Christ hath showed me."* In addition, Philippians chapter 1 verses 23-24, you will notice 'Paul being torn because his desire was to be with the Lord, which was far bet-ter for him, but he realized that he needed to be where the Lord had called him to be.' I really believe that if we are sensitive to this, the Lord will tell us when our time is.

I knew the exact hour when my mother went home to be with the Lord. This was thirty years ago, I was sitting on my couch, crying and praying because my mother was dying of cancer. I cried out to the Lord, 'I don't want her to die, I don't want her to die,' and just like that, I knew. The phone rang and it was my sister-in-law and before she spoke, I said, "Mommy just died, didn't she?" My sister-in-law was startled and said, "Oh, how did you know your mother died?" I said, "The Lord told me." and I continued to say, "I am on my way." Six weeks later, for those of you who do not know my testimony, I am sitting in the Atlantic City Medical Center with my dad who was in the hospital, and the Lord says to me, 'to live is Christ, and to die is gain; say goodbye to your father.' My mom had just died six weeks earlier. She was just 58 and my dad was 59.

I was not ready to be an orphan. I stayed as long as I could that night and I then, went home. I walked in the front door and told my husband "My dad is going to die tonight." My husband replied, "Gwen, you're in grief because you just buried your mother. You don't even know what you are saying. Just go put on your pajamas and go to bed." "No!" I said. "I'm going to stay in my clothes, because my dad is going to die tonight." He said, "You're not sleeping in your clothes." As I was submitting to my hus-band, I remember thinking to myself, "I want shoes I can slip on that have no ties; I want a shirt I can pull on that has no buttons; because the minute they call me I have got to get there." Yep, you guessed it they called that night. As quickly as possible I was dressed, out the door, and at the hospital. I arrived there in time to have my dad lay in my arms and as he was dying, I sang and priased the Lord. I prayied through his passing and he went home to be with the Heavenly Father.

That experience left me to be a firm believer that many times in the bible; people knew when they were dying so that they could gather their loved ones and make that last amends. Jacob knows he is dying and he gives his sons his final charge.

> Genesis 49:29-31 *"And he charged them, and said unto them, I am to be gathered unto my people: bury me with my father's in the cave that is in the field of Ephron the Hittite, In the cave that is in the field of Machpelah, which is before Mamre, in the land of Canaan, which Abraham bought with the field of Ephron the Hittite for a possession of a burying-place. There they buried Abraham and Sarah his wife; there they buried Isaac and Rebekah his wife; and there I buried Leah."*

Who did Jacob end up being buried next to? One might think that he would want to be next to Rachel. However, the scriptures tell us he requested to be buried next to Leah. Did Leah get exactly what she had prayed, that he would love her, dwell with her, and be joined with her? Absolutely! Who had a great end? Leah!

## Key Point

No matter what your affliction and no matter what you are going through; as Leah did, in the middle of her life, put your focus on Jesus and keep it there. Do not focus on your sorrows, but remember that Jesus is the Son of God's right hand and He loves you. He is joined to you and He dwells with you. And His Word states, 'He will never leave or forsake you.'

## Closing Prayer

*Father, thank You for the Word of God. Lord I just thank You that you have shown me that there is such a difference between Rachel's spirit and Leah's spirit. Father I want to have Leah's favorable end. As I look at what happened for Leah, and the minute she said, "I will name this boy Judah" (to God be the praise, she was fortunate, happy, blessed, and rewarded); she was lifted up to have great favor with you. Thank You for continuing to reward and bless me. As I have bowed before Your Word today and have humbled myself before Your mighty hand. You have lifted me above my afflictions with a garment of praise and with a right and pure heart. I will continually praise You. In the Name of Jesus, Amen.*

# CHAPTER 2

## *— The First Stone —*
## *The Sardius of Judah*

*Father, thank You for Your Word. Your Word is settled in Heaven even above Your Name, as it says in Psalm 138. In addition, thank You for what You are going to teach us and for what You will show us. Lord, we want more than just head knowledge or to only gain more facts. We need to know how to apply this revelation to our lives. Thank you, that in the book of Peter it says we are living stones, and a Holy priesthood. As we study the stones in the breastplate, Lord, open up our hearts, and give us ears to hear what the Spirit is saying. We ask for the anointing of the Spirit of God to make this Word relevant to our everyday life. In Jesus Name, Amen.*

What I am teaching on is the breastplate of the high priest, and I probably will say this in every chapter as part of my introduction. A couple of years back, the Lord showed me in Ezekiel that before Lucifer fell, when he was the anointed cherub, he had beautiful stones and walked in the presence of God. In the book of Ezekiel Chapter 28, the stones are named. Moreover, a couple of years ago when I was reading the book of Ezekiel, the Lord said to look at those stones. They were the same as in the high priest's breastplate, however, there is one row of stones missing. Lucifer only had nine stones out of the twelve. This is not a teaching on Satan, I want to teach about God. Once we read about these twelve stones, I will let you know what row is missing. It is unbelievably exciting!

In this chapter, we are going to look at the first stone in the first row. Therefore, if you look again at verse 17, it talks about the first row, and the first stone in that first row is the sardius. The sardius stone represents the tribe of Judah. Let me say this, almost every one of the twelve stones or the twelve tribes represents two blessings in the Bible. There is a blessing given by Jacob as he is dying. He is going to call his twelve children together and he is going to pronounce a blessing over them. Then years later, Moses prophetically speaks a blessing over each one of the twelve tribes.

> Exodus 28:15-21. *"And thou shalt make the breastplate of judgment with cunning work; after the work of the ephod thou shalt make it; of gold, of blue, and of purple, and of scarlet, and of fine twined linen, shalt thou make it. Foursquare it shall be being doubled; a span shall be the length thereof, and a span shall be the breadth thereof. And thou shalt set in it settings of stones, even four rows of stones: the first row shall be a sardius, a topaz, and a carbuncle: this shall be the first row. And the second row shall be an emerald, a sapphire, and a diamond. And the third row a ligure, an agate, and an amethyst. And the fourth row a beryl, and an onyx, and a jasper: they shall be set in gold in their enclosings. And the stones shall be with the names of the children of Israel, twelve, according to their names, like the engravings of a signet; every one with his name shall they be according to the twelve tribes."*

As you may recall, the Key Definition for the name *Judah* is "praise be unto God." This was Leah's fourth son. In addition, do you remember how everything changed the minute she took her eyes off Rachel and Jacob. All her circumstances changed. She declared, "I will praise the Lord," and from that moment on, her entire life changed.

The Key Definition for the *Sardius* stone, the first stone in the breastplate is "red" or "carnelian (redness)." The Hebrew word for *Sardius* is "Odem." The interesting thing is that the word sardius or the word "red" is the same word for "Adam." The first man God created was "red" and his name was *Adam*, which means, "taken from red clay." Really, in God, and in Christ, we are all red because of the Blood of Jesus. It is not that we are White, Black, Hispanic, or Asian; once we come to Christ, we are all covered in His blood. We are all part of a new creation in Jesus, who is also called 'the last Adam.'

While exploring the Scriptures, I found two verses that make the meaning of this stone so clear. One of the Scriptures is 2 Kings chapter 3 verses 20-23 *"And it came to pass in the morning, when the meat offering was offered, that, behold, there came water by the way of Edom, and the country was filled with water. Moreover, when all the Moabites heard that the kings were to come up to fight against them, they gathered all that were able to put on armor, and upward, and stood in the border. They rose up early in the morning, and the sun shone upon the water, the Moabites seeing the water on the other side as red as blood: they said, This is blood: the kings are surely slain, and they have smitten one another: now therefore, Moab, to the spoil."*

In the rest of the chapter, you will find that Moab is totally defeated. Here God tells Israel, 'to dig trenches, and fill them with water. When the enemy looks, they see red blood.' The interesting thing about this is they did not win the battle. If you look at the end of verse 22 it says, *"and the Moabites saw the water on the other side as red as blood."* That is the word for the sardius stone. You already know where I am going with the stone of the sardius for Judah as it represents the Blood of Jesus, and that is something we can continue to praise God for.

Isaiah 63:2 *"Wherefore art thou red in thine apparel, and thy garments like him that treaded in the wine fat?"*

The Scripture is speaking about 'putting their garments in wine and how their garments turned red; as red as blood.' Now let us get into some phenomenal Scriptures about the blessing that Jacob bestows on his son Judah. I am only going to look at three verses, and then show you details about these particular verses and thier blessing.

Genesis 49:8 *"Judah, thou art he whom thy brethren shall praise: thy hand shall be in the neck of thine enemies; thy father's children shall bow down before thee. Judah is a lion's whelp: from the prey, my son, thou art gone up: he stooped down, he couched as a lion, and as an old lion; who shall rouse him up? The scepter shall not depart from Judah, nor a lawgiver from between his feet, until Shiloh come; and unto him shall the gathering of the people be. Binding his foal unto the vine, and his ass's colt unto the choice vine; he washed his garments in wine, and his clothes in the blood of grapes: His eyes shall be red with wine, and his teeth white with milk."*

Can you see, Jacob is speaking this blessing prophetically over Judah. The book of Revelation reveals that Jesus is the Lion of the Tribe of Judah. From Jacob's blessing we see three things in verse 8. The first prophetic point about Judah and the sardius stone is that the brothers are going to praise him. When you think about Jesus and how He deserves all the praise, glory, and honor; whether you are in America, Africa, India, Romania, or wherever you are; those that love the Lord all have the same spirit of praise towards Him. Therefore, the very first thing written about Judah, praise be to God, is that *"all the brothers shall praise you."*

The second point revealed in verse 8 is that he shall have His hand on the neck of his enemy. He defeats the enemy. If someone grabs you by the neck, they have you. Have you ever watched wrestling on TV? When a wrestler puts his opponent in a choke hold, the one being held is restrained in such a way that there is a temporary disruption of blood flow to the brain, potentially rendering the one being choked unconscious. It is quite an effective way to subdue an adversary. What does the Bible say about Jesus, who is the Lion of the Tribe of Judah, *"his hand is on the neck of the enemy."*

The third point is found at the end of verse 8 where it says, *"Thy father's children shall bow down before thee."* Let me tie these points together. All the brothers shall praise you; your hand is on the neck of the enemy and every true believer desires to bow down before you. Of course, bowing down speaks of worship. There is a vast difference between praise and worship. Praise is thanking God for the wonders He has done. When you get to worship, that is pure love and adoration. Not for what He does but for who He is. That is the difference.

Praise Him for what He has done; worship Him for who He is. That comes from a heart that is in a right relationship as a child of God. Have you ever noticed a difference between praise and the worship during a service? You usually feel a significant change when the music goes from exuberance and we are singing, *"Look What Thee Lord Has Done"* to a time where you bow down because, He is Holy and He meets with you in sweet fellowship. In verse 9, it says that 'Judah is a lion; a whelp, a crouching lion, and an old lion.' Therefore, verse 9 shows us that Judah is a lion. In

Verse 10, we read, *"the scepter shall not depart from Judah."* Evidently, this tribe of Judah has a scepter. And I would say, 'the ownership of a scepter speaks of authority and kingship.

I trust you are learning something about the Tribe of Judah. Judah is praise: he has his hand on the neck of the enemy and all his father's children bow to worship him. He is also a lion and this lion is not a wimp. This lion has a scepter. I am sure we have all seen the movie *The Wizard of Oz* with the cowardly lion, nervously clutching his tail. He is always afraid. The Lion of the Tribe of Judah does not fear anything. Remember, the Bible does not say that Satan is a lion. It states in Peter, *"Satan goes around as a roaring lion."* There is a big difference between being a lion and roaring as a lion. Jesus is our Lion of the Tribe of Judah who has defeated the works of the enemy and the scepter shall not depart.

I just wanted to go over this verse with you so we can be well informed. The scepter holds authority, rules, and kingship. It shall not depart from Judah, nor a lawgiver from between his feet until Shiloh comes. The definition of *Shiloh* is "peace." In the Old Testament we see that temple was located in Shiloh and we all know that Jesus is the Prince of Peace. It is interesting that verse 10 is really a prophecy about the rapture, it says *"And unto Him shall be the gathering of the people."*

In verse 11, we see that his garments were washed in blood, *"the blood of grapes."* This is one of the reasons why some churches use grape juice for communion. The grape juice represents or relates to the Blood of Jesus. Inverse 12 the only thing we need to remember is that, *"his eyes are red and his teeth are white with milk."* That is a lot of blessing in just four verses.

Let me go into detail about each one of these things that we have looked at so far. This all relates to Jesus; there is no question about it. He is the Scepter, He is the King, He is the Lion, He is the Lawgiver, and He is the Peace of Shiloh. He is going to gather all of us to Himself. All the brothers shall praise Him and all of His father's sons will bow down to Him.

Micah 5:8 *"And the remnant of Jacob shall be among the Gentiles in the midst of many people as a lion among the beasts of the forest, as a young lion among the flocks of sheep: who, if he go through, both treaded down,and teareth in pieces, and none can deliver."*

This Scripture is saying when a lion strikes; no other opponent within the forest can withstand the terror of his attack. He is the king of beasts and the king of the forest. When watching television documentries on lions, I am so fascinated because I tend to relate them to the Bible. The lion has such power and control over their prey. They usually strike at the neck to render their prey unconscious, as they go in for the kill.

Let us look at a terrific verse that we often miss, Proverbs chapter 20 verse 2. Do you remember that the Bible says 'the enemy goes about as a roaring lion.' I am going to tell you what the roar of a lion really is. I remember the day I first saw this verse in the New International Version (NIV) where it stated *"A king's wrath is like the roar of a lion; he who angers him forfeits his life."* I am so glad that he is not going to roar over my life. In Revelation chapter 13 verse 8 when John the Beloved looked, he saw a 'Lamb that had been slain from the foundation of the world.' There are two things people are going to see in the end times; those of us who know Him and love Him are going to behold the 'Lamb slain from the foundation of the world.' Those who are left behind, who are unbelieving and have never received Him, are going to behold the 'wrath of a roaring lion.'

Have you ever been to a zoo or heard a lion's roar? I used to go and I loved to watch the zoo keepers feed the lions. As soon as the zookeeper would feed them, the lions would start roaring. The sound of their roar would echo in the arena, and you could feel the vibration of the sound. It was awesome and felt so powerful.

There is another Scripture I've found in Proverbs chapter 30 verse 30 *(NIV)* that speaks about the power of a lion. It states, *"A lion, mighty among beasts, who retreats before nothing."* Jesus is the Lion of the tribe of Judah. He roars, and nothing can stop Him. He never retreats. Every now and then, I think we give the enemy too much credit. We have to remember, we are on the winning team. We serve Jesus, who is the victorious one; He has his hand on the neck of the enemy. The only thing we need to do is serve Him and be obedient to Him. Then He will crush our enemies.

In the book of 2 Kings, 'God told the Israelites to dig ditches, and as the enemy sees the sun hit the water, it will seem like pools of red blood to them. This cause the enemy to turn on themselves. They attacked themselves from within, ran down to get the spoils and were totally defeated.' We have a powerful Lion from the tribe of Judah. He retreats from nothing.

Back in the blessing of Jacob it says, *"The scepter will not depart from his hand."* The book of Esther tells you the most about the scepter. Esther finds favor in the king's eyes, and becomes his new wife. Esther does not reveal that she is Jewish. There is an enemy in the book of Esther, and his name is Haman. I do not know if you have ever been to a synagogue. however, my son- in- law is Jewish. He told me whenever they celebrate the feast of Purim, they are forbidden to say the name Haman because he is the arch-enemy of the Jews.

Haman wanted to kill all of the Jews and plotted against them. Finally, Esther knew she had to go before the king. Here is what I want you to see, in order for you to have an audience with the king, the king has to summon you. For whatever reason, even though King Ahasuerus loved Esther and married her, he had not called for her in thirty days. Her uncle Mordecai told her, in essence, *"you have got to go to the king to stop this decree to kill our people. And, you had better tell him that you are a Jewess because you will be killed too."*

The most famous verse in this book says: *"For such a time as this."* Esther is all cleaned up; she puts on her royal robe, and stands in the inner court. Moreover, if the king does not want to see her, after she has broken protocol by coming into that inner court, they can have her stoned. The only way to know that she has been accepted is if the king extends his scepter to her. So really, the scepter represents favor with the king.

I hope you have read the book that Tommy Tenney wrote, called *Favor With The King.* This is a wonderful book. Esther chapter 5 verse 11 says *"All the king's officials and the people of the royal provinces know that for any man or woman who approaches the king in the inner court without being summoned the king has but one law: that he be put to death. The only exception to this is for the king to extend the gold scepter to him and spare his life. But thirty days have passed since I was called to go to the king.'* Do you see in this Scripture that there is an outer court, an inner court, and the Holy of Holies. Esther was able to go in to the inner court and Haman stayed in the outer court.

In addition, you can see even in the book of Esther that a scepter was made of solid gold, and it represented acceptance from the king. Because we do not live in that kind of a society, we do not really understand this type of absolute rule and authority. What did the prophecy that Jacob gave to his son Judah say, 'You'll have a scepter that will never depart from your kingdom.'

Esther 5:2 *"When he saw Queen Esther standing in the court, he was pleased with her and held out to her the gold scepter that was in his hand. So Esther approached and touched the tip of the scepter."*

When a king extends his to scepter to you, you have found favor. How glad I am that we have the favor of the Lord. In Psalm chapter 5 verse 12 it states *"For you, O Lord, will bless the righteous; with favor You will surround him as with a shield."*

Scripture speaks about Jesus having favor with God and man. I am glad to know that I have the King's favor. It is good to know that we do not have to stand in the outer court with the other people. When we want to come into His presence, He just extends that golden scepter so that we can bow in His presence with thankful hearts for His grace and favor.

In addition, there is a wonderful verse in the book of Numbers, offering more insight regarding the scepter. Additionally, this relates to the prophecy in Genesis 49 about *"being gathered"* to Him.

Numbers 24:17 *"I see him, but not now; I behold him, but not near. A star will come out of Jacob; a scepter will rise out of Israel. He will crush the foreheads of Moab, the skulls of all the sons of Sheth."*

To paraphrase the above Scripture, 'I cannot see him yet, but I can behold him.' This I know for sure, 'a star came out of Jacob, and the scepter will rise out of Israel.' Who is the scepter that will rise out of Israel? Obvi-

ously, it is Jesus. There are too many prophecies in Genesis 49 not to realize that this is talking about the 'King of Kings' and 'Lord of Lords.' Remember, we have His favor, and if you want to come into His presence, He will extend His golden scepter to you.

In Genesis 49, it says that 'Judah was a lion, his scepter would not depart, he would keep his hand on the neck of the enemy;' but it also talks about 'his garment being washed in blood.' Later it goes on to say, *"he washed his garments in wine, and his clothes in the blood of grapes."* I only picked one verse; because there were many about our garments and that, He changed them. However, in Revelation chapter 7 verses 13 & 14, the elders asked John while he was on the island of Patmos, *"These in white robes who are they, and where did they come from?" I answered, "Sir, you know." He said, "These are they who have come out of the great tribulation; they have washed their robes and made them white in the blood of the Lamb."* How many of you know that you cannot take something and wash it in blood and have it come out white.

I would like to share something that happened to me recently. I waspreaching in Lewistown, Pennsylvania. I had a message all prepared for the church. I was staying at the house of the apostle who oversees these churches, and I came downstairs to get a cup of coffee. He said to me "Did you ever think of how hard it is to get a blood stains out of clothes?" I said, "No, not at 7:30 in the morning, I haven't even given it a thought." After we had our coffee, we went to the church. The first song they sang was *There is Power in the Blood.* The second song they sang was *Nothing but the Blood of Jesus.* I am starting to think, 'Oh boy! I've got the wrong message; maybe I'm supposed to do the message on the Blood of Jesus.' During the service, a young girl shared her testimony and explained how her father had been in prison. After his release, he began sending death threats to her. She tried to get a restraining order against him. During this time, the Lord spoke to her and said, "My blood is sufficient for you." Now you know the message I had prepared went right out the window. I got up and preached on the Seven Sprinklings of the Blood. I thought how true it is that nothing could make us right except for the Blood of Jesus.

There is a story in Zachariah chapter 3 where 'Joshua stood before the

Lord, and it said that Satan stood at his right hand to accuse him of having filthy garments.' Then the Lord said to Joshua, 'I've changed your raiment; I've changed your garments.' All of us have filthy garments and we do not have any holiness or righteous of our own; however, we must remember that the Blood of Jesus has cleansed us. Trust me, I do not want to go through the Great Tribulation. I just have to tell you the truth; I do not like suffering and I do not like pain. I just want to watch everyone else and say, 'see you should have gotten saved.'

I remember as a child in Catholic School, the nuns would ask us if we would die for our faith. They said 'we need to be prepared to suffer for our Savior.' One of the nuns asked, "Would you deny Jesus?" Back then, I could not answer that question. Today, with God's grace I will not deny Jesus. I will not be like Peter, who denied Jesus. He washed our robes, He took them, dipped them in blood and they became white.

Revelation 1:14 *"His head and hair were white like wool, as white as snow, and his eyes were like blazing fire."*

All through the book of Ezekiel and the book Revelation, when they began having visions of Jesus, His eyes are flames of fire. I am glad that I do not have to worry about burning in the fire of hell. God is an all-consuming fire, and that fire is within us. The Word says he will baptize you with the Holy Ghost, and fire. When this prophecy is given, it is talking about the future and how we need to be filled with the Holy Ghost and to have the fire of God in our lives. The Scripture also mentions that 'his teeth were white with milk.' Milk in the Bible speaks about the Word of God.

Let me share three verses with you. 1 Peter chapter 2 verse 2 *"Like newborn babies, crave pure spiritual milk, so that by it you may grow up in your salvation."* Newly saved Christians must be fed simple truths. Just as newborn babies in Christ crave the milk of the Word, in the natural, newborn babies are going to crave milk every three hours.

When I raised my children, I used Dr. Spock's book on rearing children. It was like a bible, I followed it intensely. If that book said that if the baby drinks only an ounce of milk and falls asleep, you could not feed them for four more hours. My poor daughter would scream and cry for months, be-

cause she was hungry. Therefore, with my second child it was different. If he wanted a bottle, here have a bottle, have two. I think every mother should have her second child first. I really do, because we would have a lot less dysfunction. Babies desire milk and they want it all a time. In addition, if you do not give it to them, they will not have strong bones and be healthy. There comes a point where the doctor will tell you, to introduce some additional foods to the baby. We used to have this little heating dish. Now I am going back, let's see, about 40 years. The dish had sections and you plugged this dish into the wall, and it would get hot. Now the mistake I made is that if I gave my baby the cereal or the fruit before the meat she would not touch the meat ever, because it tasted so nasty it was dry like cement. She wanted something soft and easy to swallow. Yet she would never be healthy if she had not eatenthe meat.

Christians cannot live on the milk of the Word alone, because there comes a time where they need to have the substantial meat of theWord. There has to come a time when you say, "You know, I've been on the bottle long enough."

There is a problem in the church when baby Christians are inmature and choose not to grow up. It is not pleasant to meet a little child who speaks like a baby.

> 1 Corinthians 3:1-4 *"And I, brethren, could not speak unto you as unto spiritual, but as unto carnal, even as unto babes in Christ. I have fed you with milk, and not with meat: for hitherto ye were not able to bear it, neither yet now are ye able. For ye are yet carnal: for whereas there is among you envying, and strife, and divisions, are ye not carnal, and walk as men? For while one saith, I am of Paul; and another, I am of Apollos; are ye not carnal?"*

Do you see where in verse 2 he said in effect, 'I have fed you with milk and not with meat because you were too immature to swallow anything with substance?' Once you have been saved ten years, you do not need to hear sermons on salvation. You are saved, and you need to study other doctrines and begin to grow. Envy, strife, and division are all signs of immaturity. It so clear in verse 3, 'where in there is envy strife and division are you not babies?' He did want to give them meat.

Hebrews 5:12-14. *"For when for the time ye ought to be teachers, ye have need that one teach you again which be the first principles of the or-acles of God; and are become such as have need of milk, and not of strong meat."*

In the Bible, there is milk, meat, and strong meat. *"For every one that uses milk is unskillful in the word of righteousness: for he is yet a babe."* Understand that there is nothing wrong with being a baby, if you are new to the Christian faith. However after ten or twelve years have gone by, it is really time to grow up. *"But strong meat belongs to them that are of full age, even those who by reason of use have their senses exercised to discern both good and evil."*

Judah's teeth are as white as milk, which is the Word of God, but he also knows how to have the meat of the Word. I was reading John chapter 4, about the woman at the well. The disciples came back with food, and they said to Jesus, 'Are you hungry? We would like to feed you. Jesus said, I have meat, you don't know of. My meat is to do the will of Him who sent me and finish the work.' We now know what strong meat is. It is not just to start up the work; it is to finish the work. Many of us have the meat of the Word, but we do not finish the work.

Let us review the blessing Jacob gave to Judah and the sardius stone:

    1. All of his brothers shall praise Him
    2. He has his hand on the neck of the enemy
    3. People bow down and worship Him
    4. He is a lion with the scepter of authority
    5. He has washed his garments in blood
    6. His eyes are flaming fire
    7. His teeth are white with milk

This is the blessing of Moses to Judah. Deuteronomy 33:7 *"And this is the blessing of Judah: and he said, Hear, LORD, the voice of Judah, and bring him unto his people: let his hands be sufficient for him; and be thou an help to him from his enemies."*

There are a number of things written in this verse; but what He spoke to me is that he hears Judah's voice. Judah has the ear of God. God hears

Judah. I hope that as you ponder this that you realize that God wants to hear your voice and what he will hear is praise. Because that is what *Judah,* means, "to give God praise."

## Key Points

- Remember the Blood of Jesus and apply it
- Remember He is the Lion of the Tribe of Judah
- Remember to praise and Shiloh (peace) will come
- Remember to thank Him for gathering you in His arms and to bow in worship
- Remember you have the King's favor and He has extended the golden scepter
- Remember that milk is for the young in the Lord, but strong meat belongs to those who are all full age
- Remember you have been equipped to finish the work

## Closing Prayer

*Father, I thank you for the Word of the Lord. Cause me to remember that the first stone in the Breastplate is red like the Blood of Jesus. Thank you for opening my heart and helping me to realize that I have the Lion of the Tribe of Judah who no man can conquer. He has His hand on the neck of my enemies. I am so thankful that to me He is Shiloh, and He will come with peace. I know that one day I will be gathered to Him. Father, I just thank you that I hear your voice. I pray that now that I have learned about this first stone, I will be quick to give you praise, quick to bow down and honor you, and quick to worship you. Thank You that I have the King's favor. Thank You for extending the golden scepter. Thank You for giving me the Law of the Lord and that it is a light to my eyes and health to my flesh. Lord, I thank you so much for the milk of the Word, the meat of the Word, and the strong meat that will cause me to finish all that I put my hand to in the Name of Jesus. Amen.*

## CHAPTER 3

# — The Second Stone —
# The Topaz of Issachar

*Father, thank You for the Word of God. Thank You that in Your Word, it says that even though heaven and earth shall pass away your Word remains forever. Lord, we just want to thank You for Your Holy Spirit, who is going to open up the Word to our hearts. Lord, I know that these chapters on the breastplate and the stones of glory or the stones of beauty are somewhat of a challenge, but I am depending on the Holy Spirit to help enlighten the readers of this book. I just ask that you would do for us what it says in the book of Luke, "Did not our hearts burn within us, while He opened to us the Scriptures." Lord, open the Scriptures up to us and give us the ability to understand and apply it to our lives. Knowledge alone cannot help us, for the Bible says that knowledge puffs up, but love builds up. Lord we are not reading this just to get head knowledge, we are asking to have our hearts changed by Your Word. We know that Jesus is our High Priest, and He carries us on his heart, because as Peter said, we are living stones. So Lord, we thank You as we now prepare our hearts to learn about the second stone, the Topaz of Issachar. In Jesus Name, Amen.*

Exodus 28:15-21 *"And thou shalt make the breastplate of judgment with cunning work; after the work of the ephod thou shalt make it; of gold, of blue, and of purple, and of scarlet, and of fine twined linen, shalt thou make it. Foursquare it shall be being doubled; a span shall be the length thereof, and a span shall be the breadth thereof. And thou shalt set in it settings of stones, even four rows of stones: the first row shall be a sardis, a topaz, and a carbuncle: this shall be the first row. And the second row shall be an emerald, a sapphire, and a diamond. The third row a ligure, an agate, and an amethyst. In addition, the fourth row a beryl, and an onyx, and jasper: they shall be set in gold in their enclosing. Moreover, the stones shall be with the names of the children of Israel, twelve, according to their names, like the engravings of a signet; every one with his name shall they be according to the twelve tribes."*

Genesis 30:18 *"And Leah said God hath given me my hire, because I have given my maiden to my husband: and she called his name Issachar."*

The Key Definition for *Issachar* means to "receive a reward." In this chapter, we are going to find out how we are rewarded. It is interesting that the first stone is the Blood of Jesus, our salvation. When we look at the second stone, we will see there is a reward for those who are God's children. We are going to look at a very familiar story in Genesis, where we find a man named Abram. God is going to tell him to look at the stars in the night and the sand and sea.

Moreover, that is how many children he is going to have. When God comes and tells him this, Abram had no children at all. We shall start in Genesis 15 because the actual Hebrew word for *Issachar* is found in verse 1, *"After these things the word of the LORD came unto Abram in a vision, saying, Fear not, Abram: I am thy shield, and thy exceeding great reward."* God calls, Abram, the first man He is going to bring into covenant, and He is going to give him a reward. So many people are trying to do this or that to be rewarded, but God said him, *"Don't be afraid, I am your shield and your great reward."* Now, what was it that Abram was rewarded with? Let us get to the actual blessing of Issachar.

Ezekiel 28:13-14: *Thou hast been in Eden the garden of God; every precious stone was thy covering, the sardius, topaz, and the diamond, the beryl, the onyx, and the jasper, the sapphire, the emerald, and the carbuncle, and gold: the workmanship of thy tabrets and of thy pipes was prepared in thee in the day that thou wast created. Thou art the anointed cherub that covereth; and I have set thee so: thou wast upon the holy mountain of God; thou hast walked up and down in the midst of the stones of fire.*

Please do not forget that the whole reason for reading this book is to learn about how Lucifer had only nine of the twelve stones. He was missing one complete row, as we have seen in our readings of Ezekiel 28. By the time you reach the end of this book you will see ever so clearly, what the enemy does not have. I am so excited about what the Lord has revealed to me.

We know that Abram eventually had children, so that obviously was part of his reward. Nevertheless, there was something far greater in Abram's life that God gave him as a reward. God said to Abram *"I am your shield, and I am your exceeding great reward."*

Follow me as I share with you some of the details of this story. This is the first time in the Bible that you see the ceremony to cut covenant. In verses 10 and 11 of Genesis 15, they would 'select an animal and cut it down the middle, laying the two pieces of the animal rib cage to rib cage, leaving a space between those two bloody carcasses. The next step would be that the two men were going to make covenant and they would walk in a figure eight, making pledges and promises to each other.' Here is where God comes in and decides to cut His own covenant with Abram. This is far better than cutting it with any man because God cannot make a mistake. God put Abram into a deep sleep. 'As he is sleeping, it became dark, a smoking furnace and a burning lamp appeared in these things.' Remember, this book is not a teaching on the blood covenant, but the reward that Abram received and it was that God cut a blood covenant with him. That is the great reward.

Genesis 15:17-18: *"And it came to pass, that, when the sun went down, and it was dark, behold a smoking furnace, and a burning lamp that passed between those pieces. In the same day, the Lord made a covenant with Abram, saying, unto thy seed have I given this land, from the river of Egypt unto the great river, the river Euphrates."*

Because of the world we are living in today, the great majority of people break their covenant with God. The divorce rate right now for people in the church has become the same as those within the world. It is a sad thing, but I believe that one out of every two marriages ends up in divorce. People who are married stand before God making a covenant *"until death do us part."* People must stop and take a moment to understand what they are saying along with the importance of the vows they are making.

When you cut covenant with God, He expects you to keep your word. He keeps His always. Let us say you went to Africa, where there was a king of a tribe who was your ally. You and the king would cut your skin, mingle your blood, and then you would put dirt in the wound that would leave a marking. Once you were marked, you could never get that mark off. If you went into a village where there were people who wanted to take your life showing them this mark or scar, they would not harm you, because you had favor with the king. That is how important a blood covenant is for us. Thank God we have been marked with the Blood of Jesus. Even when the enemy comes, greater is our God; so much greater is our King. We are forever marked for God.

After a considerable amount of research, I really do not have anything profound to say about the topaz stone. What I will say is that the color of this particular stone is a greenish yellow. In the book of Job it says, 'the topaz is the stone of Ethiopia.' I am more interested in the man who is on the stone, because of the reward we receive. As I have mentioned previously let's look again at the blessing of Jacob and the blessing of Moses. All the patriarchs, the twelve sons of Jacob, received a 'blessing from their father on his deathbed.' Later on, they received a 'prophetic utterance from Moses' in the book of Deuteronomy. To briefly re-cap what we have covered so far in our reading; the blessing of Moses to the tribe of Judah was about the lion who was a King and would rule with a scepter. Moreover, it was hundreds of years before Jesus came on the scene. Isn't it great how the Word of God is so inspired and so infallible.

Looking at the blessing of Jacob there is no question that you will figure out what the reward is. There is something said about the tribe of *Issachar*. His name again means "reward." There are things that are in this chapter that pertain solely to him and how he ties into the second stone on the breastplate.

> Genesis 49:14-15 *"Issachar is a strong ass couching down between two burdens: And he saw that rest was good and the land that it was pleasant; and bowed his shoulder to bear, and became a servant unto tribute."*

Do you see that these verses state Issachar is going to be a real strong donkey? If you look throughout the Bible, you will see that these animals were loaded with burdens. They did not have all the beautiful horses that we have today. Even to this day, some people who go on these escapades through the Grand Canyon (I'd much rather look at postcards) hire mules. You pile your supplies, your water, food, etc. on this beast of burden and you would pull this beast of burden through the Grand Canyon. The donkey becomes your burden bearer. Looking at Issachar and again at verse 14, *"he is a strong burden bearer, strong between two burdens."* Issachar is a tribe that can handle burdens. I do not know about you, but sometimes we can be burdened down, and not know what to do.

Last year on Palm Sunday, I preached an unusual message at church about being a donkey for Jesus. I went into the whole purpose of the donkey in Jesus' life on Palm Sunday. Jesus came to His disciples and said, *"Find me a donkey or a colt that has never been ridden. Go get it and bring it to me."* There was the miracle of Him getting on a wild untamed donkey. The whole ministry and purpose of this particular donkey was to lift Jesus higher. I had such a message from God on this truth; leaving me with the thought of, we all need to be donkeys for the Lord. Why would we need to be a donkey? Just to make sure that everyone sees Jesus high and lifted up; also, so that all men are drawn unto Him. You and I can learn how to bear our burdens, how to have hope in a world where people are hopeless, and how to have joy in a place where people are depressed. We have the same burdens they have. Not all of us have perfect children. Not all of us have happy marriages. Not all of us are healthy individuals. Not all of us have money. However, there is not much that is different; except that we have a burden bearer. Issachar is a strong mule that can thrive between two burdens.

I want to share with you about a burden. Before we get to the reward, we need to know how to deal with our burdens. Here is what I have found out, you can have a burden from the Lord, and then you can just have a burden. When God gives you a burden as in the book of Jeremiah, you will know the difference. God has only given me a couple of burdens that I knew were from Him.

When this happens, it is all you think about as these types of burdens become all consuming; to pray for someone or to call someone, there is no getting away from it. You will go to bed with it, you will wake up with it, and until you do something about it, that burden does not lift. You cannot cast it away and you cannot rebuke it away.

Jeremiah had such a burden for God's people. He is known as the weeping prophet. There are many verses in God's Word on burdens; what really causes a burden? There are many things that I could have written about, but I wanted to use what the Lord showed me in Job chapter 7 verse 20 because I think that the core of this is sin. I do not think Adam had a burden in the Garden of Eden, do you? There were no thorns, no weeds, and no thistles. I mean, the man took a nap and woke up married. Moreover, when he looked at Eve, he said 'Wow, man, woman.' Before the fall and before sin, there were no burdens. Now because of sin, humankind has all kinds of burdens; sometimes we can bring them on ourselves. True?

I remember years ago, a couple came over to our house for some financial counsel. We helped them balance their checkbook, and we helped them set up a budget. Finally, after working with them for close to a year, they had decided that they were going to upgrade their car. Now, we spent a long time going over their finances to help them figure out what size payment they could afford. We checked out their insurance, all the costs for the tags and the registration. In short, we figured out that the monthly payment they could afford would be approximately $300.00. My husband and I stood in our foyer, we prayed for them to have wisdom and that they would not be taken advantage of. It was about an hour later, they pulled up into our driveway in a new car, beeping their horn. They had bought a brand new car with no money down. The payment was $529.00 a month, and they could afford only $300.00.

After that day, they could not understand why they began to feel burdened. If I had ever wanted to slap someone, it would have been them. I said, "You brought this burden on yourselves. You knew what you could afford and you overextended yourself. Over a period of time, due to a combination of problems, they actually lost their house and moved back into a room in their mother's attic. Some of the burdens we have, we deserve, because of unwise decisions we have made.

Job 7:20 *"I have sinned; what shall I do unto thee, O thou preserver of men? Why hast thou set me as a mark against thee, so that I am a burden to myself?"*

Psalm 38:4 *"For mine iniquities are gone over mine head: as an heavy burden they are too heavy for me."*

Sometimes, burdens come about because of our sin. The minute that you know that you have such a burden you need to go to the Lord for help.

Psalm 55:2 *"Cast thy burden upon the LORD, and he shall sustain thee: he shall never suffer the righteous to be moved."*

I am sure that all of us can acknowledge that we have sinned and made some unwise decisions, but if we repent and turn to God, He will help us. He will bring us out of our burden and free us from our sin.

For those who know me they know that I am not a fisherman; however, my dad was. He made me go fishing one time and can I just say, 'It was the most boring experience I ever had in my whole life.' We sat in this little tin boat, in the middle of a lake, in the hot sun, and he would not let me eat my crumpets. I had taken a package of Tasty Cake crumpets and my thermos. All day long, I asked my dad if I could eat my crumpets because I was bored. I had to just sit in this boat holding a fishing pole for hours, and nothing happened. At that moment, I decided that I would never go fishing again! Guess what I have been true to my word.

It is my understanding that a good fisherman will practice casting. I do not exactly understand but I remember watching a movie called *A River Runs Through It,* with Brad Pitt, and all he did in the movie was practice casting. As a result when I thought about casting this Scripture popped into my head; *"cast all your cares upon the Lord."* You know, the first time you cast your cares; they will probably drop right at your feet and trip you up by nightfall. However, if you keep practicing casting your cares upon the Lord, as the burdens get bigger and bigger they will be easier to release. We have to be consistent and begin with the smaller burdens, so that the bigger burdens will not be so hard to cast. Remember, whenever any little annoyances or burdens are in the way, try casting them away. Cast it and leave it! You do not cast something, and then go see how it is doing. You have to learn to forget about it. It seems as though we have a tendency to cast our burden and then real it back in to see how it is doing. Cast your cares and burdens on the Lord and leave them with Him.

If you are under a burden that you cannot deal with and it feels as if it is crushing you, I would encourage you to fast. Fasting is something that many people do not talk about anymore; however, God says in Isaiah 58 that "we should fast." In this particular Scripture, you will see many promises; even if you only turn down one meal, you become eligible to claim these promises for your life. You do not have to start with a three-day water fast, just start by skipping one meal, and spend that time in prayer seeking God. In this verse, you see that God is 'talking about His chosen fast.'

Isaiah 58:6 *"Is not this the fast that I have chosen? To loose the bands of wickedness, to undo the heavy burdens, and to let the oppressed go free, and that ye break every yoke?"*

I do not know of a verse that promises more power, punch, and freedom then this Scripture. Let me break this down for you.

1. He is going to undo any wickedness or sin in our lives
2. He is going to lift any heavy burdens that we have
3. If there is any oppression, He will set you free from the oppression
4. If there is any yoke, He is going to break it for us

Once you break the yoke, it is shattered. There is no putting it back together. This is what God wants to do for us. Just like *Issachar,* there are two burdens, a natural burden, and the burden of the Lord. When you have a natural burden, or a burden that is self-inflicted, it is important for you to learn how to cast your burden upon the Lord. The Lord wants to lighten our burden. He did for Issachar, and He wants to become that strong part of our life, which can carry those burdens without us crumbling under the weight.

Please do not wait until it is a millstone decide to start while it is still a pebble. Turn to the Lord and say, "Please take care of this for me, I do not know what to do about this; Lord, I need your direction." We should all take the time to learn the Scripture in Matthew below.

Matthew 11:29-30 *"And Jesus said, take My yoke upon you, and learn of Me; for I am meek and lowly in heart: and ye shall find rest unto your souls. For My yoke is easy, and My burden is light."*

Do you know what a yoke is? A yoke is a wooden beam placed between a pair of oxen to allow them to pull a load. Often two oxen would be yoked together. An older, more experienced ox would be teamed up or yoked with a younger, less experienced ox. The older ox in the yoke is the "strong authority" who, through being yoked together, teaches the younger ox. The stronger ox would bear the weight of the whole burden. Jesus said, *"My yoke is easy."* Therefore, we have to make sure we stay connected. We have to make sure that we follow Him and that we do not try to have Him follow us around. The little ox does not have the strength or the ability to tell the stronger ox where to go. Jesus is our burden bearer. If we can stay in step with Him and stay yoked to Him, He will bear the weight of any strain in our life.

I have had several eye surgeries in the past and the outcome has been somewhat disappointing. During that time, I became discouraged and had to turn to the Lord, I saying, "Lord this is a burden, I need my eyes, I need to see so I can read, study, and write." When I would read something, my vision would blur and I would develop a headache. I learned that I needed to follow my own teaching and cast my burden and give it to the Lord by saying, "Lord I trust You, You are my vision and I chose to let go of this daily burden." Giving the Lord all of the praise and glory, it was not long after that prayer that I began to see a little clearer; I can now read without a headache.

Genesis 49:15 *"And he saw that rest was good and the land that it was pleasant; and bowed his shoulder to bear, and became a servant unto tribute."*

*Issachar* was a servant, and I would like to show you some of the rewards of being a servant of God. First, we come to Jesus (Judah, sardius where we are covered by the blood); the very next thing we are supposed to do is become a servant. A servant bears burdens, a servant carries things, and a servant does whatever the master tells them to do. Therefore, what is *Issachar?* He is a servant, and his name means "to be a rewarded." I want you to know that if you serve God you will be rewarded. Will you always get the reward in this lifetime? I think not, but you will be rewarded. I know what I want to hear one day, "Well done, good and faithful servant."

The New Testament has much to say about servant-hood. We are going to look at four Scriptures on becoming a servant. Jacob is the one who declared these blessings over *Issachar*, 'that he would bear burdens and that he would be a servant.' This parable has been on my heart for a long time. Before, I never really paid much attention to it. I knew it was in the Bible, but it was not really speaking to me; however, now it is speaking volumes. I found this fact to be very interesting, the phrase, *"The Lord's servant,"* is found 885 times in the Bible. I went onto one of the Bible research websites and typed in the word "servant" and 56 pages came up on that topic.

Luke 17:7-10 *"But which of you, having a servant plowing or feeding cattle, will say unto him by and by, when he is come from the field, Go and sit down to meat? In addition, will you not rather say unto him, Make ready wherewith I may sup, and gird thyself, and serve me, till I have eaten and drunken; and afterward thou shalt eat and drink? Doth he thank that servant because he did the things that were commanded him? I think not. So likewise ye, when ye shall have done all those things which are commanded you, say, we are unprofitable servants: we have done that which was our duty to do."*

Let me put this into plain words. Say you hire someone to cut your grass. After they are finished, they come in and ask you "I would like dinner now, oh, would you please wash my hands, and serve me." I think not! Listen, you would say, "You're working for me today. You take care of me and then afterwards you can have your meal. After all, you're the servant and I'm the master." The verse continues to say, "Hooray, you did great! You're so wonderful!" In the chapter above He said, "no, rather you should say, I only did my duty." That is it, "I just did my duty." A good servant will not make a show out of their servant-hood they just simply obey.

John 12:26 *"If any man serve me, let him follow me; and where I am, there shall also my servant be: if any man serves me, him will my Father honor."*

Here is another Scripture that ministers to me; it is where Jesus washed the disciple's feet. He says, "If I, your Master have done this, how much more should you do? If I set an example, what will you do?" You know when the Lord asks us to do something for Him; there is nothing we cannot do! That is quite a Scripture. If we serve God, the Father will actually honor us. There is one thing that we need to be very mindful of when it comes to servant-hood.

John 13:16 *"Most assuredly, I say to you, a servant is not greater than his lord; nor is he who is sent greater than he who sent him."*

We should never get to the place where we think the servant is greater than the master. As servants, we must stay humble. Christ exalts the lowly.

The last Scripture I wanted to give you about being a servant is found in 1 Corinthians. I am not talking about slavery here when I am talking about servant-hood. There is a big difference between respecting someone who serves you and actually degrading another person.

1 Corinthians 7:22 *"For he that is called in the Lord, being a servant, is the Lord's freeman: likewise also he that is called, being free, is Christ's servant."*

To be a servant of God is to be free, to be a free man. It has nothing to do with someone making you do what they want you to do. He has given us a free will. It is really a privilege to serve Him. What happens to servants? They are rewarded! The first thing that you and I do after we receive Jesus is we can become servants. I never found my fulfillment in Christ until I actually began to serve Him. I have a good husband. As well as I have two healthy children, a girl and a boy. You look at people and you think why would they take their life? Why do they do drugs or why would they get drunk? Because, in the book of Ecclesiastes it says, "there is a hole in every heart of man, yearning for eternity." I think the least I could do is serve Him and in doing so serve Him with all my heart.

Let me share a story about my grandson, Luke. While I was away ministering, my son, who pastors, called me during my drive home. He said, "Mom, something wonderful happened in church today." I said, "What happened?" He replied, "Luke got saved!" I said, "Oh, put him on the phone." Luke (who was five at the time) gets on the cell phone and I said, "Luke, it's Mom-mom, I heard you gave Jesus your heart." Wait this is best part of the story, this little five-year-old boy replied, "Mom-mom you're wrong, I did not give Jesus my heart. I gave Jesus my life." I had to pull over on the side of the road, because I started to cry, and thank the Lord. Too many people just give Him their hearts, but keep their own life. What a life lesson for me. People do whatever they want with their lives, whenever they want to do it, yet what God really wants is for us to serve Him joyfully.

We have seen what Jacob's fatherly impartation and blessing over Issachar is; now let us look at what the spiritual blessing is. One blessing was more natural, and the other blessing is supernatural or spiritual. The blessing of Moses over Issachar is in:

Deuteronomy 33:18(b)-19 *"And of Zebulun he said, Rejoice, Zebulun, in thy going out; and (b) Issachar, in thy tents. They shall call the people unto the mountain; there they shall offer sacrifices of righteousness: for they shall suck of the abundance of the seas, and of treasures hid in the sand."*

The first stone, represents the Blood of Jesus whereby we are saved, and we praise God. The second stone is where we become a servant, and all of us who serve God will one day be rewarded. In the blessing bestowed from Moses to Issachar, we see that they offer sacrifices of righteousness. When we begin to serve God, we start to make sacrifices. You cannot really serve anyone or anything, if you are not willing to make a sacrifice. Our sacrifice is of righteousness. Again, do not let the word righteousness fool you. People use the word righteousness, and they think of a schoolmarm all dressed in black, who never laughs, or enjoys herself. The word *righteousness* means "being in right standing with God." Jesus made us righteous. It says, "Jesus was made unto us wisdom and righteousness." When you are in right standing with God that is what it is to be righteous. As we serve Him, we bring to Him sacrifices of righteousness.

I would like to show you a couple of Scriptures that deal with the sacrifices of righteousness.

Psalm 118:19-20 *"Open unto me the gates of righteousness, and I will go in and I will praise the Lord: this gate of the Lord into which the righteous shall enter."*

Evidently, not only do we make sacrifices of righteousness, but there is also a gate of righteousness we have to enter into. The way to get into that place with God can be found in Psalm 100. The way to enter through the gate of righteousness is by thanksgiving.

Psalm 100:1-5 *"Make a joyful noise unto the LORD, all ye lands. Serve the LORD with gladness: come before his presence with singing. Know ye that the LORD he is God: it is he that hath made us, and not we ourselves; we are his people, and the sheep of his pasture. Enter into his gates with thanksgiving, and into his courts with praise: be thankful unto him, and bless his name. For the LORD is good; his mercy is everlasting; and his truth endures to all generations."*

*Issachar* is a servant who offers sacrifices of righteousness, opening the gates of righteousness, and we entered through those gates in thanksgiving. Finally, the last Scripture for this particular blessing of Moses is in the book of Hebrews. I do not know if you know this, but I was never able to memorize anything. I mean, I am still working on my times tables; I think I should just quit and get a calculator. So, when I would hear people quote Scripture I would wonder, how did they ever memorize all of those verses? I would try to memorize them and I was awful at it. Psalm 100:1-5 was one of the first Scriptures I wanted to memorize. What I have found in my life is that I am better if I meditate upon the Scripture, than if I try to memorize it. You see, there is a difference between memorization and meditation. Memorization is a deliberate, repetitive mental process. It is undertaken in order for us to store information so we can recall that information later; however, meditation is a spiritual discipline.

In Philippians, we are to *"meditate on whatever is true, whatever is noble, whatever is admirable; if anything is excellent or praiseworthy."* In other words, 'think on these things, ponder them, and digest them.' When I learned to do that, I became so amazed when I would hear the Scripture come out of my mouth. Because I had not memorized them, I had meditated on them. Hebrews chapter 13 verse 15 is one of them.

Hebrews 13:15 *"By Him therefore let us offer the sacrifice of praise to God continually, that is, the fruit of our lips giving thanks to his name."*

What is the sacrifice of righteousness? It is the sacrifice of praise, continually. I was not naturally a thankful person, I just felt like life had dealt me some hard blows. I was never thankful. I felt that everyone owed me and I was going to get you before you could get me. I was a very hard, angry woman. After the Lord melted my heart and saved me I thought, what else could I do except give the Lord thanks and praise.

Psalm 34:22 *"The LORD redeemed the soul of his servants: and none of them that trust in him shall be desolate."*

Psalm 35:27 *"Let them shout for joy, and be glad, that favor my righteous cause: yea, let them say continually, let the LORD be magnified, which hath pleasure in the prosperity of his servant"*

Gods desire for you is to be prosperous. He really wants us to have prosperity, which is a wholeness and wellness in every area.

Acts 2:18 *"And on my servants and on my handmaidens I will pour out in those days of my Spirit; and they shall prophesy"*

Romans 6:16 *"Know ye not, that to whom ye yield yourselves servants to obey, his servants ye are to whom ye obey; whether of sin unto death, or of obedience unto righteousness?"*

Romans 6:22 *"But now being made free from sin, and become servants to God, ye have your fruit unto holiness, and the end everlasting life."*

## Key Point

A true servant will bear another's burden, and do whatever the master tells them to do. A good servant will always be rewarded, in this life or the next.

## Closing Prayer

*Father, I thank you for the Word of God. Lord, help us to learn the basic lessons of Issachar, that as Your servants we will be rewarded. I pray that we would keep a servant's heart and that You would help us not to be arrogant, proud, self-seeking, or boastful. Lord Jesus, You are the greatest Servant of all. You laid down your life for us, how much more do You ask us to do the same. Lord, you said that Issachar could bear two burdens and be strong. Therefore, I pray that when we are overcome by burdens, You would give us the ability to cast all of our burdens and cares upon You. Because You care for us. Jesus, I pray now that we would see ourselves yoked to You, not in slavery, but side by side, serving You. I pray that we would be able to follow You as You lead and guide us into that which is good for our lives. Open for us the gates of righteousness so that we may know that we have a right standing with You. I am so glad to be able to offer a sacrifice of praise, in Jesus Name, Amen.*

## CHAPTER 4

# –The Third Stone –
# The Carbuncle of Zebulun

*Father, I would like to thank You for the Word of God. I thank you that the Bible tells us that everything we need for life and for godliness has been given to us through the knowledge of the Scriptures. I ask that You would open our hearts and our minds so that we would be able to understand Word of God. In the book of James it states, "if anyone hears the word and does not do it, he deceives his own heart." Lord, we know that the Bible says that we are living stones. As we continue to learn about the breastplate and we look into the stone of Zebulun, the carbuncle, we asked for wisdom, insight and revelation so that we could live what we have learned. We are not interested in book knowledge or head knowledge only, but that our hearts would be converted and changed in order to bring You glory. In Jesus Name, Amen.*

I would like to give you a quick recap of the first two stones. In row one we are on the third stone of the breastplate of the high priest. Again, you know that Hebrew is read from right to left. The very first stone we studied is the stone called the sardius and if you remember, it was the color of blood red. The tribe associated with the sardius is Judah. I am excited about the first stone and to know that Jesus is the Lion of the tribe of Judah. Once I was saved, the blood of the Lamb covered me. We could never be living stones, nor could we be a kingdom of priests unto our God, unless we are covered by the Blood of Jesus. To me it is very efficient how the first stone represents the blood of the Lamb. The second stone we studied was the topaz. That was the stone of Issachar, and it represents the reward reserved for anyone who serves God. As we follow the stones in their order, we discover that every stone holds meaning that can be applied to our lives.

First, we are born-again and we accept Jesus. Then we are covered by the blood and praise God. We become servants with a servant's heart and when we serve God with a right heart, attitude, and motives, He will reward us for our servant hood. Now we are going to complete the first row of stones. The third stone is called the carbuncle and it represents the tribe of Zebulun.

Let us go back to Genesis Chapter 29. Where Zebulun got his name and what it means. Then we will review the Key Definition for the carbuncle stone.

Genesis Chapter 29 lists all the twelve tribes of the children of Israel. We see that Jacob was the father of these twelve men who became the twelve tribes of Israel. Remember, in the first chapter we saw how Leah never felt loved.

Genesis 31:18-20 *"And Leah said, God hath given me my hire, because I have given my maiden to my husband: and she called his name Issachar (Issachar is the second breastplate stone, and his name means, 'be rewarded.') And Leah conceived again, and bare Jacob the sixth son. And Leah said, God hath endued me with a good dowry; now will my husband dwell with me, because I have born him six sons: and she called his name Zebulun."*

The Key Definition for *Zebulun* is, "to dwell with honor" or "to dwell together." In this chapter, we will a look at what it means to dwell.

Now let us put the stones in order:

1. First we are saved
2. We become a servant
3. We dwell with the Lord

The Key Definition for the *carbuncle* is "glittering lights." Once again, first, we are saved and we praise God for the blood. As we begin to serve Him, He rewards us. As we dwell in Him, we start to live in the light. Now

I want to show you what it means to dwell in Him and walk in the light.

Psalm 91:1-4 *"He that dwelleth in the secret place of the Most High shall abide under the shadow of the Almighty. And I will say of the LORD, He is my refuge and my fortress: my God; in Him will I trust. Surely, He shall deliver thee from the snare of the fowler, and from the noisome pestilence. He shall cover thee with His feathers, and under His wings shalt thou trust: His truth shall be thy shield and buckler."*

Let us look at what it means to dwell in the secret place. I do not know about you, but I have a special place in my home where I really like to do my Bible reading, have my devotions, and pray. It is like my secret chamber. I would like to show you what the secret place is it is found right here in this Psalm. What does it mean to dwell in the secret place? When you are dwelling it does not mean that you are running here or running there or joining this or doing that. It means that you are inactive. It means that you are going to sit down, take a deep breath, and dwell with the Lord. It says that there is a secret place when we dwell with Him. I really believe that the secret place is found in verse 4 of Psalm 91. It says that, *"He will cover you with His feathers, and under His wings, you shall trust."* In verse 1 it talks about the shadow of the Almighty. Throughout the Old Testament God said that He would meet with His people, tabernacle, and dwell with them. He said that he would meet them between the wings of the cherubim or between the feathers of the angels that were on top of the mercy seat. To gain access to my secret place, I start by thanking God for his mercy because it speaks about Him meeting us there; dwelling with us between the wings the cherubim, between these angels wings spread out over the mercy seat, where the Blood of Christ was sprinkled. I do not know how you do your devotions, but if you have been doing this for a long time you to need to know the origin of why you do it. You do not want just to be monotonous and repetitive about your process. The secret place is under the wings and Jesus said, *"As a hen I want to gather you under my wings, but you would not."* We have free will and I do not know about you, but when Jesus spreads out his wings, I want to be under them. I want to be tucked in tight and close to Jesus. You know that the eagle has a very massive wingspan and in the book of Isaiah it says that we will, *"mount up with wings as the eagle,"* and we would *"run and not be weary."* Did you know that an eagle will spend from one to three hours every morning preening its feathers? An eagle's wingspan measures from 6 to 8 feet. In addition, an eagle will apply oil from it's preen gland (also called the uropygial gland), which is located at the base of the tail. The bird will squeeze the gland to extract the oil and then work the oil into its feathers. This oil cleans and waterproofs the feathers, and deters parasites. When you see an eagle swoop down to catch a salmon, it goes right down into the water and catches that salmon and lunch is served. I often wondered how they could fly if their wings were wet but you see, they have already prepared for this. Wouldn't it be good if we prepared for some of the storms that life hits us with?

I believe the secret place for me is under the shadow of the Almighty. Under His wings is my secret place. He promised many times in the Old Testament to dwell and meet with us, tabernacle with us under the wings of the cherubim at the mercy seat. Aren't you glad that He did not say that He would dwell with you at the judgment seat? I am glad for us that He said He would meet with us at the mercy seat.

Psalm 140:13 *"Surely the righteous shall give thanks to Your Name; the upright shall dwell in your presence."*

It is not enough just to go to the mercy seat in your mind or go under the shadow of the Almighty, or under the wings, or into a secret prayer closet, if we do not have His presence. I am sure that you know that sometimes you do not sense the presence of God. It does not mean that He is not there; but there are other times, when it is as if He is waiting for you. You have no sooner said, "Good morning, Lord" or started your prayer when His presence is right there. Those are the times it is hard to leave. It does not happen every day, even though I wish it did! There is something awesome about the presence of God. The Word of God says, 'not only do we dwell in the secret place under the shadow of the Almighty, but also the whole purpose is to dwell in His presence.' The third Scripture I want to look at is Isaiah chapter 32 verses 17-18. I have really used this Scripture sense my salvation. When I was a younger woman and my children were at home I remember one time my daughter and I had an argument. She ran upstairs and slammed the bedroom door. I stood at the bottom of the steps and screamed this verse up to her. So, I've known this verse for about 20 years and I have really worn it out.

Isaiah 32:17-18 *"And the work of righteousness shall be peace; and the effect of righteousness quietness and assurance forever. And my people shall dwell in a peaceable habitation, and in sure dwellings, and in quiet resting places;"*

Whenever we would have a family issue, I would cite that Scripture. *"I dwell in a peaceable habitation, a place of quiet, rest, and assurance."* So let us look at the Scripture where it says, *"my people shall dwell in a peaceable habitation."* Just know,that you that when you have stuff going on in the house and everybody is getting uptight and you start to become stressed, try to get a hold of this verse. Write it down somewhere because we need peace in our homes; there is nothing worse than strife and discord. I know I am supposed to focus on dwelling, but the Scripture talks about dwelling in His presence and dwelling in peace. Remember these three things: First, we dwell in the secret place. Second, we are in the secret place to get into His presence. Third, the fruit of His presence will be peace.

During a Bible study, one time, we got into a discussion on strife. I recalled a conference I was invited to speak at where the topic was resolving conflicts. I thought to myself, I am the wrong speaker. I do not resolve conflicts. I run and get a bag of potato chips or pretzels and munch all of my anger away until the people are done fighting. Then I come back and sing peace like a river. I spoke to the pastor and he said, "We have been praying, and we know you're the one." So afterwards, I agreed to speak at that conference; I knew the Lord was stretching me. The Lord is not one to keep us in our comfort zone. I remember seeking the Lord and saying, "Lord, I don't even know how to do this, so how can I teach this?" Then the Lord gave me one Psalm that changed everything for me.

Psalm 80:6 *"Thou makest us strife unto our neighbors: and our enemies laugh among themselves."*

What a powerful verse. We are talking about God's peace, God's presence, and about the secret place. I realized that when I let strife into my life, obviously, I lose my peace. Our peace goes right out the window. When that Psalm came to me years ago, it was around Halloween. I remember going shopping and I was walking through one of the stores that sells scary decorations. One of them had a very scary, demonic laugh when I passed by. As I heard it laugh, I said to the Holy Spirit, 'Every time I get into strife, would you remind me that this is how the enemy laughs?' I do not want to hear the devil laughing and I certainly do not want to hear goblins laughing in my house. We would be willing to say, "Okay, I yield whatever it takes, let's make peace and let's somehow resolve this." Therefore, when we dwell in the secret place, in His presence, we dwell in peace. *Zebulun* means, "to dwell with honor." I will say this concerning Leah, when Jacob was about to die, he said, "I want to be buried nearest to Leah." She did get what she asked; by naming her son *Zebulun,* "to dwell with honor," she asked that her husband would honor her and that they would dwell together.

Let us look at a couple of verses about the light. Remember the Key Definition for *carbuncle* is "brilliant light."

The Bible says that we were once in darkness but now we are children of the light. It speaks of how we have to cast away deeds of darkness and put on the armor of light. It is very important that we bring everything into the light. In fact, in Hebrews chapter 12, it mentions that everything is open and naked before Him to whom we have to give an account. So do we really think we could hide things and get away with it? It's not happening. The sooner we bring it into the light, the better it is. I remember hearing a speaker say, "We are as sick as the secrets we keep." That really spoke to me. I can tell you, to the best of my knowledge, I do not have any skeletons, and I do not have any dark areas that I am trying to hide. I want everything out into the light because He is in the light. In Genesis, do you know that God created light before the sun and the moon? He did this because it was Jesus who is the light of men. I remember one time I was looking at Genesis and I read He created the light. Then it said on such and such a day he created the sun and the moon. I thought, what was the light he created? Well, it was Jesus. He is the light of the world so we could walk in light. This next verse will help us to remember to stay in the light because He is in the light.

Psalm 56:13 *"For thou hast delivered my soul from death: wilt not thou deliver my feet from falling, that I may walk before God in the light of the living?"*

Now, unless you remember what it was like to be in darkness, you might not appreciate the light. I remember what it was like when I was a child of darkness. I thought I was a good person. I never murdered anybody. I thought I was a Christian, but I was not. I was in darkness. I remember having this tremendous fear of death. It tormented my mind. I use to envision my daughter in a coffin when she was three months old and what outfit I would put her in if she died. Then every couple of months I would change the outfit in my mind; if my baby died, I would envision different outfits to bury her in. Then I had my son and would pick out little suits for him. It was not until I was saved that I realized that this tremendous fear of death and darkness really had a hold on me. I use to ask people, "Will you come to my funeral?" I was in my twenties and I remember one time going to a co-worker's house. I met her mother and my first conversation was, "Listen, if I die, will you come to my funeral?" And she said, "Absolutely not!" I was 22 years old and I ran out of the house crying. I use to tell my husband, "I want you to leave my eyelids open in the coffin. Find a mortician that will keep my eyelids open. I want them stitched open." All of these weird, weary, and demonic thoughts were upsetting. Then I came to Christ and all of a sudden, I experienced what it says, *"the people who sat in darkness have seen a great light."* All of those thoughts and statements stopped. No more visions of coffins and I never again had dress rehearsals in my mind of what my children would be buried in at their funeral. I intend to live as long as the Lord has me here on earth. I have no fear of death whatsoever. I have no darkness in my life. I know that absent from the body means to be present with the Lord and I have been delivered from the spirit of fear of death. I want to tell you that I know what it is to be in darkness. I am so thankful for the light, for every single day that we have light in our lives. Therefore, we are to walk before God in the light. The more light we have and the more we walk in God, the easier it is to serve Him and the greater the reward. I do not know about you but this is not a burden to me. My only regret is that I waited until I was 27 years old. I wish my salvation had come as young person.

God is merciful so we need to walk before Him in the light. Look at Psalm 119. It is the longest Psalm in the Bible with 176 verses.

Psalm 119:105 *"Thy word is a lamp unto my feet and a light unto my path."*

So how do we walk in the light? We walk in the Word. The Word is a lamp unto my feet. The more Word we have, the more light we have in our lives. Do not tell this to my grandsons, but when they come over, they like to scare my husband. I live in a wooded area so it is pitch dark in my house. We pull the curtains, we turn off the lights, and Jake and Luke are just shaking and quaking because they want to scare Pop Pop. I bought them little headbands that have lights in them; if you could only see them, running through the house with a light here there! Every time they turn a light out, they would be scared or stumble. Isn't it the same with us? Every time we walk in darkness, we stumble. One of the worst things a woman can do is move the furniture and not tell anyone. My mother would do this all the time. I used to sneak out and sneak in and I would have the whole living room memorized. Then she would move a piece of furniture around and bang! I would wake up my parents and get into all kinds of trouble. I said, "Mother, would you stop changing the furniture around?" Now you know that that was not the issue. The issue was me. I did not have a flash light. Once you turn the light on, darkness has to flee. Now, it is not enough to have a lamp. You have to have batteries or oil because you need something to keep the light fired up.

Psalm 119:130 *"The entrance of thy words giveth light; it giveth understanding unto the simple."*

I hope you are not offended if I call you simple. I am not calling you simple minded. You know, sometimes we have to have simplicity. There was one verse, in the book of Colossians, which caused me to meditate for many years. I could read it but I could not understand it. Psalm 119:99 says, *"I have more understanding than my teachers do because I meditate your word."* Therefore, this verse was a challenge for me. I kept saying to Him, "Please help me understand this verse. Please give me insight. Please give me wisdom. Please open my heart." Now I understand the verse.

The entrance of God's Word gives light and understanding to the simple. I was told as a kid that I was forbidden to read the Bible and that I would not understand it. When I was saved, a Methodist Minister handed me a *New Testament Living Way Bible.* It was a paperback with pictures, but I handed it back to him. I told him I could not understand that, he said, "It was the Living Way; you can't get anymore paraphrased than that." I said, "No I can't, it's the Holy Book." Moreover, we went back and forth because he wanted me to read it. Finally, the pastor said to me, "Are you illiterate?" I got upset and exclaimed, "No, I am not!" He proceeded to ask, "So, why don't you want to read this?" I replied, "I was told I would not be able to understand it." He said, "Just take it home and read a couple of chapters in John and see if you can understand it." Now, all these years later, I am still devouring as much of the Word as I can get. Only when you come simply and say you need light will you understand it. We have all been around intelligent people. I mean, they have a fabulous IQ. They have more letters behind their name than one would care to mention, but you know sometimes they just seem to miss the small stuff and do not get it. You just have to become very simple. Just take a moment and let Him know that you are a simple woman, or a simple man, a simple child in Christ – just open the Word. This is how we get light and understanding. In order to see, you have to keep that battery charged so you can understand it.

Isaiah 9:2 *"The people that walked in darkness have seen a great light: they that dwell in the land of the shadow of death, upon them hath the light shined."*

How glad I am that His light has shined on us. If we are going to dwell with the Lord in His presence, then we have to be truthful, open, and honest. We have to bring everything into the light.

I can think that I have my house clean, by using Windex and Lysol for the counter leaving everything looking nice until the sun shines in the window. When the light comes in, you can see things that you had not seen before. Even though it is daylight, there is just something about that bright light. Have you ever had the Lord do that to you? He just shines this bright light and you realize, "Oh, I didn't know all of that was in me! I thought I was pretty good and clean," until He put the light on.

The word *Zebulun* means to "dwell with honor." We have to walk in the light before God and we have to use the Word as a lamp. The way we refuel the energy is to keep the lamp lit through understanding the Word of God. We have to pray to understand it because the light has shined upon us, and our goal is to dwell with Him and bring Him honor.

Genesis 49:13 *"Zebulun shall dwell at the haven of the sea; and he shall be for a haven of ships; and his border shall be unto Zidon."*

It is interesting that the first thing Jacob says is how Zebulun shall dwell and where is he going to dwell? He is going to dwell in a haven. Jacob pronounced this blessing upon Zebulun. It is going to be a haven for ships. I had to understand that a haven is "a sheltered place of refuge." This takes us back to Psalm 91. If we get under the shadow of the Almighty, He will be our shade and our protection. Once you and I dwell in the presence of God and let His light flood our lives we are going to be in a sheltered place, a haven. In addition, we become like a place of rest for people who do not have the peace that we have.

Deuteronomy 33:18-19 *"And of Zebulun he said, Rejoice, Zebulun, in thy going out; and, Issachar, in thy tents. They shall call the people unto the mountain; there they shall offer sacrifices of righteousness: for they shall suck of the abundance of the seas, and of treasures hid in the sand."*

What is Zebulun going to rejoice about? Remember, he is a haven for ships. He is going to rejoice because he is going to be given treasures; hidden treasures. I am excited to let you in on a secret, God has hidden treasures, and when you find a nugget, jewel, or a gem, it is so invaluable. How do you find your treasure? If we dwell in the light then we have a shelter of refuge, we become a safe harbor, and we have treasures within us. On the television, they have shown the treasures that have been brought up from old shipwrecks. The value of these things are incredible. We have something more valuable than that. I have something more valuable than a whole case of rubies, diamonds, emeralds, and every other gem you might think of. It is right here and it is the Word of God. This is a treasure. There is a verse that says, *"We have this treasure in earthen vessels so that the all surpassing power and greatness would be of God and not of us."* You have treasure inside of you. They may be hidden and buried but they are in your life. I challenge you to find out what the hidden treasure are in your life. The Word of God is like a treasure map. The pirates of old had a map and they would try to find the treasure using landmarks. We can uncover and enjoy the treasure God has for us if we search in His Word.

Isaiah 33:6 *"And wisdom and knowledge shall be the stability of thy times, and strength of salvation: the fear of the LORD is his treasure."*

Look at the way the stock market is going crazy, all the insane political things that are going on, the price of gas, and the struggling economy. Look at what this verse says, *"Wisdom and knowledge will be the stability of your times."* Isn't it good to be stable? No matter what is going on, we trust in the Lord and He takes care of us. This verse is beautiful. He actually says that the *"fear of the Lord is His treasure."*

I have been in some churches where there was no fear of God whatsoever and it really bothered me. There are certainly some extremes. As a Catholic, I was brought up with so much fear to include fear of the altar, the priests, and the nuns. You could not talk in church and if you crossed your knees, you were hit with a ruler. You were only allowed to cross your ankles.

Yet sometimes we have a tendency to go too far the other way. When I first got saved and I found out that Jesus was my friend, we became buddies. All of a sudden, He reminded me that He was the Son of God and the fear of the Lord began to come back to my heart. I am very grateful for that. If you are lacking in the fear of the Lord, just start reading the Scriptures about those who God punished and you will straighten out real quick.

Mathew 6:19-21 *"Lay not up for yourselves treasures upon earth, where moth and rust doth corrupt and where thieves break through and steal: But lay up for yourselves treasures in heaven, where neither moth nor rust doth corrupt, and where thieves do not break through nor steal: For where your treasure is, there will your heart be also."*

Therefore, whatever you value, whatever you treasure, that is what has your heart. God is saying do not treasure all of the things of the earth that are going to be burned up one day. Treasure things of eternal value because where your treasure is, there your heart is.

Matthew 13:44 *"Again, the kingdom of heaven is like unto treasure hid in a field; the which when a man hath found, he hides, and for joy thereof goeth and selleth all that he hath, and buyeth that field."*

Here is a person that finds out that there is a treasure in a field and he sells everything he owns to buy the field where the treasure is hidden. Go back to the gold rush. Look at what all the people did just to get a nugget. They thought a nugget was a great treasure and when they found it, they had great joy. When the Bible speaks to you, doesn't it bring joy into your life?

2 Corinthians 4:7 *"But we have this treasure in earthen vessels, that the*

*excellencies of the power may be of God, and not of us."*

You have a treasure inside of you, all of the power of God. You do not get the credit. You do not get the glory. It all belongs to Him. There is a treasure in an earthen vessel. Remember, it is not the vessel that is valuable, it is what's inside.

Colossians 2:1-3 *"For I would that ye knew what great conflict I have for you, and for them at Laodicea, and for as many as have not seen my face in the flesh; That their hearts might be comforted, being knit together in love, and unto all riches of the full assurance of understanding, to the acknowledgement of the mystery of God, and of the Father, and of Christ; In whom are hid all the treasures of wisdom and knowledge."*

I do not know about you, but I am on a treasure hunt. I want stability in my life. I want the fear of the Lord. I need wisdom, knowledge, and understanding. If we can get those treasures in our lives, the treasure of Christ will be able to accomplish more than we had ever hoped or thought. The Bible says the God will do exceedingly and abundantly above all that we ask or think according to His mighty power that works in us.

## Key Points

The word *Zebulun* means, "to dwell with honor" and the *carbuncle* means, "glittering light." Remember, to walk in the light before God and to use the Word of the Lord, which will light your way. Also that the way we refuel the energy and keep the lamp lit is by praying for understanding. You will know His peace because the light has indeed shined upon you.If we dwell in the light, then we have a shelter of refuge. We become a safe harbor. Then within us are His treasures.

## Row One

The Sardius: Judah

> • Because of the Blood of Jesus, we can give praise to God

The Topaz: Issachar

> • You are rewarded for service

The Carbuncle: Zebulun

> • We dwell in the light

## Closing Prayer

*Father, I just want to thank You for this first row of stones. Lord, as I look at the first three stones, I am reminded that Judah means praise be to the Lord God for the Blood (sardius). I thank You, Lord, that as I serve You, I will be rewarded. I want to thank You that in Jesus are hidden all the treasures of wisdom and knowledge. Help me to have a Godly fear and reverence for You so that I will always remember that it is not the vessel, it is the treasure within. Father, I have this treasure in an earthen vessel that the all-surpassing excellence of power would be of You and not of myself. I ask you to prepare me Lord, to be in that state where I can dwell with You in that secret, quiet, peaceful place. Lord, I pray Isaiah 32:18 over myself and the Body of Christ: especially as they read this book that your people would live in peaceable habitations, in places of quietness and rest. I just lift up my home to You, Lord, and ask that there would be a prevailing sense of peace, that there will not be strife and that the enemy would not laugh at my family or me. May I continually know that one of the treasures I have in God is Your peace. I just want to thank You that I no longer walk in darkness, but I am in Your marvelous light. In Jesus Name I pray, Amen*

# CHAPTER 5

## – The Fourth Stone –
## The Emerald of Reuben

*Father, we thank You that You watch over Your Word to perform it. We thank You that the entrance of Your Word gives light and understanding even to the simple. Therefore, we thank You that because of Jesus and His Blood, we can serve You and there will be Your reward as long as we dwell in the light even as He is in the light. Father, we ask that the Holy Spirit would open our hearts and our minds. We pray that not one seed of God's Word will fall by the wayside and that we won't let the cares of other things choke it out, we won't let the birds of the air take it from us. We will hide this Word in our heart so that we will not sin against You. Lord, we know that Peter tells us that we are a royal priesthood, a holy nation, that we are living stones called out of darkness into Your marvelous light. Therefore, Father, may we understand the emerald and may we understand the tribe of Reuben. Impress on us what You have to say to each of us in Jesus Name we pray. Amen.*

Exodus 28:17-21 *"And thou shalt set in it settings of stones, even four rows of stones: the first row shall be a sardius, a topaz, and a carbuncle: this shall be the first row. And the second row shall be an emerald, a sapphire, and a diamond. And the third row a ligure, an agate and an amethyst. In addition, the fourth row a beryl, and an onyx, and a jasper: they shall be set in gold in their enclosing. Moreover, the stones shall be with the names of the children of Israel, twelve, according to their names, like the engravings of a signet; every one with his name shall they be ac-*

*cording to the twelve tribes."*

We have been moving right along and now we are on the tribe of Reuben. Looking at the origin of the name Reuben, this happens to be the emerald (my favorite stone) means. So let us go to Genesis 29. However, because this is the firstborn, it is very important we go back. The morning after the wedding, when Laban had pulled the switcheroo, so to speak, and the sun came up, all of a sudden Jacob realized that he did not have the beautiful young Rachel; he is married to her older sister Leah. The Bible does not describe anything about her figure or her intelligence. The Bible just says that she had weak eyes. The Bible says that Rachel was well-formed and beautiful to look at, so I can obviously assume, Leah was not as attractive. However, we learned in the first chapter that beauty is from within, not only on the outside. In addition, Leah became a beautiful woman throughout the story, and beautiful Rachel became envious, jealous, and angry. She named her children, 'I am going to judge against you' and 'I have wrestled and prevailed against my sister.' Given the choice of the two women, we see that even though Leah had a hard beginning, Leah ended up being honored, respected, and buried next to her husband Jacob.

Let us start with the Key Definition for *Reuben,* which means, "behold a son", or "behold a firstborn son."

Genesis 29:31-32 *"And when the LORD saw that Leah was hated, He opened her womb: but Rachel was barren. And Leah conceived, and bare a son, and she called his name Reuben: for she said, Surely the LORD hath looked upon my affliction; now therefore my husband will love me."*

Earlier, if you remember in verse 31 I mentioned, that I did not know if her sister hated her or her husband hated her, but someone hated her. If you look at verse 32, you see it was her husband. Because in verse 31 when the Lord saw the Leah was hated, He opened up her womb, Leah conceived and bore a son, and she called his name *Reuben,* for she said, *"surely the Lord has looked upon my affliction now therefore, my husband will love me."* I just think that is such a sad verse. I often tell young women the last thing you need to do in an unhappy or unstable marriage is to bring a baby into the situation. If you are having problems in your marriage, and you think that having a baby or yet another is going to make your husband love you, you are gravely mistaken.

First, fix the problems and then have children. So many women think, 'If I can just get pregnant, then he will marry me. If I can just have another baby, he will not leave me.' Leah says more or less, 'well maybe now my husband will love me.' I would like to give you a couple of interpretations. In Genesis, verse 32 it says, *"the Lord saw my affliction,"* however, according to NIV which states, *"the Lord beheld my misery."* If you look at the Amplified Bible, it goes a little further and says, *"When the Lord saw my humiliation and my affliction."* We can understand how she felt humiliated by the circumstances that had happened to her.

Every woman wants to feel that her husband loves her, wants her, and respects her. No one wants to feel like they are second class or just a left over, which is how Leah felt. God saw into her heart, and saw that she was troubled. He saw that she was in pain, and as the Amplified version said, He actually saw that she was *"afflicted with deep humiliation."* So one thing He did to soften that pain is He helped her to conceive a child. In the Hebrew or Jewish culture, it is very important to have a male child as a firstborn. The firstborn is entitled to a double portion and the firstborn will actually becomes the head of the family when the father passes away. He will be able to get more inheritance and divide it among his brothers. We are not really studying this right now, but to be a firstborn son puts you in a place of elevation. Therefore, the name *Reuben* means, "Behold a firstborn son." Now you know, and I know that all of this we are studying relates to Jesus. Obviously, He is Judah, He is the servant, and He is the firstborn.

There are certain verses in the Bible that are just so powerful, yet they seem to only be related to a certain holiday or certain time of the year. In Isaiah chapter 9, you find one of those particular Scriptures. In addition, I want you to see what God has given us. God named Leah's son Reuben to note the firstborn, but God gave us far better than Reuben. He gave us his only Son, His Firstborn, beloved Son.

Isaiah 9:6-7 *"For unto us a child is born, unto us a son is given: and the government shall be upon his shoulder: and his name shall be called Wonderful, Counselor, The mighty God, The everlasting Father, The Prince of Peace. Of the increase of his government and peace there shall be no end, upon the throne of David, and upon his kingdom, to order it, and to establish it with judgment and with justice from henceforth even forever. The zeal of the LORD of hosts will perform this."*

When you read this verse, I do not understand why people do not realize that Jesus is God. How many Everlasting Fathers can there be? There is one. I want to know how many Mighty Gods are there? There is one. Here even before He was born this prophecy was given, hundreds of years before the birth of Jesus it says that 'this Mighty God is going to become a Son for us.'

Let us look at the stone, which is the emerald. In case you did not know, the emerald stone is green. The darker the green the more valuable the stone. I have an emerald ring. The stone is so tiny, you really cannot see it, but it is an emerald. Do not tell my husband, because I was very thankful when he got it for me over 30 years ago. There is something unique about the green stone mentioned in the book of Revelation, so much so that it is mentioned twice in fact. The emerald is very rare in the Bible. The emerald appears in the book of Ezekiel and again in Revelation.

Revelation 4:1-3 *"After this I looked, and, behold, a door was opened in heaven: and the first voice which I heard was as it were of a trumpet talking with me; which said, Come up hither, and I will show thee things which must be hereafter. And immediately I was in the spirit: and, behold, a throne was set in heaven, and one sat on the throne. And he that sat was to look upon like jasper and a sardine stone: and there was a rainbow round about the throne, in sight like unto an emerald."*

Did you notice that behind the throne of God there is going to be an emerald rainbow? It is very important because of what the rainbow represents. *"He said there was a rainbow around the throne like an emerald,"* so the throne has a green rainbow around it. Begging the question what is the significance of a rainbow? Why did it not say there were emerald stones or possibly an emerald circle? I had to ask Him, "God, why is it an emerald rainbow?" If we look at Genesis chapter 9 we see the significance of why the rainbow surrounds God's throne is an emerald. I cannot wait to see that one day, I just think it will be breathtaking. The things that we value so much here are going to tread underfoot when we get there. God has a completely different system regarding what is valuable.

Genesis chapter 9 was right after the flood. I do not know if you know why God caused a flood in the day of Noah. It was because men were so violent that God repented and became very sorry for the creation of man.

The Bible said that the earth was filled with violence. You know we are never going to be covered again in water, but look at our world and you see the violence. Did you notice the news recently, where three teenagers just beat a man almost to death, leaving the young man to have a heart attack and almost die? He was only 36 years old, when they asked these kids why they did it, they responded, "we just wanted to see what it felt like to beat somebody." I have my own opinion, I think this ties back to video games, DVDs, and the things kids are watching. It is full of horrific violence. What happens if they keep exposing themselves to this type of violence they will become desensitized. How can that not be tied back to Satan?

I thought how awful, that we live in a world where you cannot walk to the train station or go to a bus stop without fearing for your life. Just look around! It is like the days of the flood. God made a promise, so we need to look at what this rainbow of emerald green signifies.

Genesis 9:11-15 *"And I will establish my covenant with you, neither shall all flesh be cut off anymore by the waters of a flood; neither shall there anymore be a flood to destroy the earth. And God said, This is the token of the covenant which I make between me and you and every living creature that is with you, for perpetual generations: I do set my bow in the cloud, and it shall be for a token of a covenant between me and the earth. And it shall come to pass, when I bring a cloud over the earth, that the bow shall be seen in the cloud: And I will remember my covenant, which is between me and you and every living creature of all flesh; and the waters shall no more become a flood to destroy all flesh. And the bow shall be in the cloud; and I will look upon it, that I may remember the everlasting covenant between God and every living creature of all flesh that is upon the earth. And God said unto Noah, This is the token of the covenant, which I have established between me and all flesh that is upon the earth."*

The symbol of a *rainbow* represents "a promise or token of a covenant." The reason for the rainbow behind the throne is that every time it is seen by us we behold the Son, we are going to remember that he made a covenant or a token with us. Not only did He make a covenant, but also, He signed this covenant in His own blood. They talk about somebody making a last will and testament, well Jesus wrote it, died and signed it in

His own blood. The emerald rainbow behind the throne will always reminds us that God made a promise to us and our whole fate rests upon the covenant, and the promises He made. Therefore, the rainbow is the covenant of a promise.

If we look at the other places the emerald appears in the book of Revelation it speaks about the temple of God, or the city of God that is going to come down from heaven like a bride. In Revelation chapter 21 verse 19 it speaks of 'the city of God having a foundation of emerald.' In verse 19, it also states 'the emerald is actually listed as one of the foundation stones for the New Jerusalem, the Temple of God and the house of God.' Not only does the rainbow remind us that we have a covenant promise, but it has become also our foundation.

Revelation 21:19 *"And the foundations of the wall of the city were garnished with all manner of precious stones. The first foundation was jasper; the second, sapphire; the third, a chalcedony; the fourth, an emerald…"*

Do you understand that all the foundation we stand on and have the house built on, along with the apostles and prophets, all goes back to God's Word? If He promised it, and He said He will do it, He is good for His word. I am so glad He is not a man, that He should tell lies. The book of Numbers tells us that men lie. How many of us have gone into a contract or a covenant with somebody? My father owned a business. He was a mechanic, over in the inlet in Atlantic City, New Jersey, where he had his own mechanic shop. If somebody brought his or her car in for repair, my dad quoted a price. He did not need a notary and three witnesses. My father stretched out his arm and shook hands with the customer. And that was it! A handshake was my father's word and you could take it to the bank. Whatever my father said he would do by that handshake. How sad it is today that we do not honor contracts and covenants; but God does. That is the good news that the emerald represents the rainbow of the covenant with all the promises that are our sure foundation.

Each tribe has a blessing from their father Jacob, as well as a spiritual impartation from their father, Moses. If we look first at the natural, in Genesis 49 he does not say too much about Reuben. Genesis 49 verse 3 is the blessing of the patriarch Jacob to his firstborn son Reuben. *"Reuben, thou are my first-born, my might, and the beginning of my strength, the excellency of dignity and the excellency of power. "*

Did you happen to notice that every now and then we read verses were he calls himself Jacob and in the same sentence, he calls himself Israel? Here is an example. He says, *"come here, you sons of Jacob and hear what Israel would have to say."* Now in case you are not familiar with this, when Jacob tricked his brother Esau and lied to his dying father Isaac, he ran and went to hide at his uncle Laban's home, where he had an encounter and he actually wrestled with God. Now it is years later and the reason he went back was to be reconciled with his brother Esau. When he left, Esau said to him, *"I'm going to kill you."* Their mother came in and said to Jacob, 'just run away until I get your brother to calm down. He's really angry because of his birthright.' Therefore, twenty years have gone by and now Jacob is returning to face Esau. Jacob was so afraid that he sent out Leah and her kids; followed by Rachel and her kids; finally Jacob brings up the rear.

What happened was that God had changed Esau's heart. Esau was ready to reconcile with Jacob. However, Jacob did not know that, so the night before this event Jacob wrestled with an angel. We have all read the story in Genesis chapter 32; 'he actually gets into a contest where he wrestles with an angel.' He tells the angel, *"I won't let you go on until you bless me."* He was blessed by having his name changed. Not only did the angel bless him by changing his name, but also he actually touched the hollow of Jacob's hip. Jacob lived with a limp for the rest of his life. To this day, the Jews do not eat the shank or the thighbone because of what happened to Jacob. Here is the issue; his name was *Jacob*, "deceiver, conniver, and trickster, the man." Once he had an encounter with God, his name was changed from Jacob to Israel. The name *Israel* means "prince of God." That is how he was blessed, God changed his nature, and God changed his character. That is what happens to us. There is no question that I was Jacob before I became a Christian. When I met God and wrestled through with all the issues in my life, He changed me. Now I have His divine nature inside. As we read the Scriptures, you will see that when Jacob is walking in the flesh, he calls himself Jacob. When he is walking in the spirit or saying something that agrees with the Word or something prophetic, he will call himself Israel. This is why he says, gather my sons of Jacob in the natural because Israel is going to speak. Now here is what he has to say to Reuben his firstborn son.

Genesis 49:3 *"Reuben, thou art my firstborn, my might, and the begin-ning of my strength, the excellency of dignity, and the excellency of power."*

Can you see, Reuben receives quite an outstanding blessing? The Bible says, *"he is the son of my strength, the son of my might, and he is my firstborn."* Then he goes on to say he is going to be excellent in power. However, hang on and watch how Reuben is going to lose all of this. Continuing on, read verse 4 and see what his father says about him.

Genesis 49:4 *"Unstable as water, thou shalt not excel; because thou wen-test up to thy father's bed; then defilest thou it: he went up to my couch."*

Reuben is going to lose his dignity, his excellency, his preeminence, and power because in this verse he committed a horrific sin. I wonder if one verse is being spoken by *Israel,* "the Prince of God," who would want Reuben to excel in dignity and power, and maybe the next verse is being spoken by his father, Jacob saying, *"you are as unstable as water, you will not excel."* If you do not study the Bible, this would look like a complete con-trast would it not? How could one verse say that you are going to excel in strength, might, and power; and the next verse say you are not going to excel?

I hope you are still following along. Let us see what he did that ruined his leadership, dignity, and respect. Reuben did something that was so of-fensive and sinful. In Genesis 35, remember that Rachel dies in childbirth. She gives birth to a son named *Benoni,* meaning "son of my sorrows." Jacob says, you will not call this son (his twelfth and last son) Benoni; we are going to change his name to *Benjamin,* meaning "son of my right hand." Look what happens right after Rachel's death. Jacob was probably grieving; because, he had a heart for Rachel since the first day he saw her. I believe Rachel died for stealing household gods. Because when she fled from her father Laban, she took his idols, and when he came to look for them, she put them in the camel's saddle and sat on them. She said to her father that it was the cycle of the month for her as a woman so she could not get up. Because of these idols, I believe this was when a curse was pronounced. It most likely was a curse of death. Watch what happens next.

Genesis 35:20-22 *"And Jacob set a pillar on her grave, which is the pillar of Rachel's grave to this day. Then Israel journeyed and pitched his tent beyond the tower of Eder. And it happened, when Israel dwelt in that land, that Reuben went and lay with Bilhah his father's concubine; and Israel heard about it."*

What you need to know right now is that Reuben, the firstborn, had sex with his stepmother. Therefore, he was not going to excel in dignity, or excel in power. He was not the one who would be in line to rule and reign. I thought well, okay, the order of birth for these men was Reuben first, then Simeon and Levi and then Judah. For him to go and lay with his stepmother, his father's concubine was such an insult and a slap in his father's face. In Genesis 34 after several sons were born, Jacob had a daughter named Dinah. Dinah ends up being raped, by a man named Hamor of Shechem. Nevertheless, what happened to her two brothers? Now remember, I have a purpose in sharing this. How did the eldest three brothers become disqualified and allow the fourth born son, Judah, to enjoy the blessings of the firstborn?

Reuben had been disqualified for his immorality. Levi and Simeon went and told the Gentile men in the town of Shechem that if they really wanted to marry the Jewish women, they would all have to become circumcised like the Jewish men. Then they would be able to marry into the Jews' families and our women into your families. It was a setup. It was a painful set up at that. So all these adult men became circumcised. On the third day when they were sore, Levi and Simeon came and killed every single one of them. Because of this sin, they too were disqualified and Jacob was furious. This is why these first three sons never became the head of the tribes. Reuben was sexually immoral and Levi and Simeon had issues with anger, which we will study when we get to their chapters. How is it that the first stone is Judah and not Reuben; because, Reuben was caught in sin just as his brothers Simeon and Levi. Let me tell you something that I found very interesting about the tribe of Reuben; this is unbelievable; there are no kings, no priests, and no prophets, ever, in the line of Reuben.

When you read the Old Testament it will be like this, one is of the tribe of Dan, one is of the tribe of Asher, and one is from the tribe of so-and-so. However, from the tribe of Reuben, because of this sin, no one came into leadership as a king, or a priest, or a prophet. Let us look at Jesus, as the firstborn Son. Let me explain to you how Judah, actually took the firstborn position. Let us look at what the Bible says about Jesus, and how He keeps his preeminence, even though Reuben did not keep his position. The word *preeminence* means "to hold first place" or "to stay in first place." Therefore, even though Jacob told his son that, he would excel as the firstborn in dignity and might; because of Reuben's free will, he became unstable and was no longer honored in that position. I took some time and reviewed some New Testament Scriptures about Jesus being the firstborn son. Jesus was perfectly moral, and never sinned. He maintained His preeminence.

> Colossians 1:18-19 *"And He is the head of the body, the church, who is the beginning, the firstborn from the dead, that in all things He may have the preeminence. For it pleased the Father that in Him all the fullness should dwell,"*

As you can see from Colossians chapter 1 verse 18, Jesus is the firstborn and He has held this position. He is the head of the body, the church. He is the beginning, the first born in all things and He has preeminence. Again, the word *preeminence* means, "to stay in first place to hold that position."

> Romans 8:28-29 *"And we know that all things work together for good to those who love God, to those who are the called according to His purpose. For whom He foreknew, He also predestined to be conformed to the image of His Son, that He might be the firstborn among many brethren."*

Therefore, just as Reuben was the firstborn among many brothers in the natural, Jesus is the firstborn among many brothers in the spiritual. I do not want to get on the doctrine of predestination, but this verse just tells us that once I receive the Lord, I am predestined to be conformed to the image of his Son. It says that 'God knows who is going to receive Him, and for those who do, His plan is that we be changed into the image of the Son.' Why do scholars sit around and debate predestination, the election, and sanctification?

Just love Him, read His Word, and serve Him! Seems too good to be true, I know. We are predestined to be more like Jesus. Is that not our goal? Should Jesus tarry, I hope we become more and more like Him, firstborn among many brothers. There was a time when the life of every firstborn male was threatened. When the children of God were in Egyptian slavery

Pharaoh tried to kill all of the first born sons.

Hebrews 11:28 *"By faith he kept the Passover and the sprinkling of blood, lest he who destroyed the firstborn should touch them."*

Every firstborn child in all of Egypt is going to die in one night, unless they put the blood of the lamb on the door. If they put the blood of the lamb on their doorpost then any firstborn in that house would live. If you are a firstborn, aren't you glad for the blood. How are the firstborn protected? By the blood. How are we protected? By the blood. If it were not for the blood of Jesus, we would not have the protection that we have. Jesus sprinkled His blood for us and His blood keeps us safe. We are all firstborn, because Jesus is firstborn among many brethren.

Hebrews 12:22-24 *"But you have come to Mount Zion and to the city of the living God, the heavenly Jerusalem, to an innumerable company of angels, to the general assembly and church of the firstborn who are registered in heaven, to God the Judge of all, to the spirits of just men made perfect, to Jesus the Mediator of the new covenant, and to the blood of sprinkling that speaks better things than that of Abel."*

Years ago, the Lord gave me a teaching on the seven sprinklings of the blood of Jesus. You can see in 1 Peter that we have become the elect.

1 Peter 1:2 *"According to the foreknowledge of God through the sanctification of the Spirit unto obedience and the sprinkling of the blood of Jesus."*

When I read that phrase, *'sprinkling of the blood,'* I started an in-depth study and found that there were seven sprinklings of Jesus' blood. Seven is the number of perfection. The reason I am saying all this is because of the tense used in Hebrews chapter 12 verse 24. It does not say you have come to the blood of Jesus that has spoken. That would be past tense. It does not say that we now come to the blood of Jesus that will speak. That is future tense. This verse actually says that we have come to *"the blood of Jesus that speaketh,"* and that is the present tense.

If you know the story of Cain and Abel, you remember that Cain killed his brother Abel in the garden. God walked into the garden and said, *"Where is your brother Abel?"* Cain replied, *"he was not his brother's keeper."* Then God said, *"I hear the voice of your brother's blood crying out from the ground."* Here is the point; in the garden, God stopped right in His tracks because He heard the blood of Abel, crying out from the ground. What do you think God does when He hears the blood of His Son speaking? How powerful is that! In the Amplified Version, it says *"we have come to the blood of Jesus that speaks mercy, not to the blood of Abel crying out for vengeance."* How glad I am that Jesus is our firstborn among many brothers that He willingly shed His blood for us. We do not have to fear the wrath, vengeance, or punishment of God. Jesus bore it all for us.

Deuteronomy 33:6 *"Let Reuben live, and not die; and let not his men be few."*

In this Scripture, we read about the blessing Moses spoke over Reuben. Because Jesus has redeemed us and we have, his covenant to stand on we will never be few in numbers nor will we ever die.

## From Row One

1. The First Stone: Sardius of Judah
   ◆ We are covered in the Blood

2. The Second Stone: Topaz of Issachar
   ◆ We are rewarded for being His Servant

3. The Third Stone: Carbuncle of Zebulun
   ◆ We dwell in the light

4. The Forth Stone: Emerald of Reuben
   ◆ We are the Beloved of God

## Closing Prayer

*Father, I thank You for the Word of God. Lord, I thank you that Jesus is indeed the firstborn among many brothers. Thank you that in the book of Hebrews it states that He is not ashamed to call us His family and that He actually is our brother. Lord, I thank You that through the sprinkling of the Blood we have been redeemed, sanctified, and delivered. I thank You that in Jesus we will never die. For I know that You have delivered us from the dead. Death is the last enemy that one day will be defeated; for all of us who believe we can say, "Oh death, where is your sting?" I know that the Bible teaches me that to be absent from the body is to be present with the Lord. I thank You that just as Moses spoke over Reuben, we will never die because we have received eternal life. I want to thank You and praise You for all You've done and will continue to do, in Jesus Name, Amen.*

# CHAPTER 6

# *– The Fifth Stone –*
# *The Sapphire of Simeon*

*Father, even though this is a deep word that you have given me to share, I know that the Holy Spirit of God can enlighten us and illuminate us by opening our hearts and minds to the truth. Let everything that is written on these pages do Your perfect work in us. I thank You that Your word is powerful and I ask that You send the truth of change into our hearts, right now, in Jesus mighty Name. Amen.*

We are going to look at row two, stone two of the breastplate of the most high priest, which is the sapphire of Simeon. He is the second son of Jacob and Leah, as we see in Genesis chapter 29. The Key Definition for *Simeon* is, "to be heard."

Genesis 29:33 *"And she conceived again, and bare a son; and said, because the LORD hath heard I was hated, he hath therefore given me this son also: and she called his name Simeon."*

We have adequately covered how Leah felt hated by her husband Jacob and by her sister who was so jealous. So *Simeon* is her second son with Jacob, and as we mentioned before, it means, 'the Lord has heard me.' Simeon's stone of glory on the breastplate of the high priest is the sapphire.

Exodus 24:9-10 *"Then went up Moses, and Aaron, Nadab, and Abihu, and seventy of the elders of Israel: And they saw the God of Israel: and there was under his feet as it were a paved work of a sapphire stone, and as it were the body of heaven in his clearness."*

In this powerful verse Moses, and Aaron, Nadab, and Abihu see the glory of God. In the very beginning of the Bible, even before the breastplate of the most high priest, is mentioned in chapter 28 of Exodus, we see the sapphire stone. It states that under the feet of God there was a pavement made of sapphire. Sapphire is the color of heaven in His clearness. Now remember, the sapphire stone appeared before the breastplate of the most high priest. It is what God walked on because it was a pavement of sapphire. The Key Definition for *sapphire* is, "polishing, to be polished." I found this incredible Scripture as I was studying in the Book of Lamentations.

> Lamentations 4:7 *"Her Nazarites were purer than snow, they were whiter than milk, they were ruddier in body than rubies, and their polishing was of sapphire:"*

Here is what I learned from this verse. The polishing of the sapphire produced a Nazarite. The Nazarite is one who God polished as a sapphire. Therefore, before we get to the blessing of Jacob or of his son Simeon, we definitely have to look at the Nazarite. The bottom line is that this teaching must be implemented in our lives. We study so that we will find ourselves approved. There is actually a chapter in the Bible that talks about the Nazarite vow.

We are going to look at some of the people who took the Nazarite vow. For some reason, we have in our mind that a Nazarite has to be a man. However, as you study Numbers you will find that a woman can take the vow of separation, just as a man could. The Key Definition for the name *Nazarite* is, "A consecrated one who is devoted or someone who has consecrated their life to be devoted to God."

> Numbers 6:1-8 *"And the LORD spoke unto Moses, saying, Speak unto the children of Israel, and say unto them, When either man or woman shall separate themselves to vow a vow of a Nazarite, to separate themselves unto the LORD: He shall separate himself from wine and strong drink, and shall drink no vinegar of wine, or vinegar of strong drink, neither shall he drink any liquor of grapes, nor eat moist grapes, or dried. All the days of his separation shall he eat nothing that is made of the vine tree, from the kernels even to the husk. All the days of the vow of his separation*

*there shall no razor come upon his head: until the days be fulfilled, in the which he separated himself unto the LORD, he shall be holy, and shall let the locks of the hair of his head grow. All the days that he separated himself unto the LORD he shall come at no dead body. He shall not make himself unclean for his father, or for his mother, for his brother, or for his sister, when they die: because the consecration of his God is upon his head. All the days of his separation he is holy unto the LORD."*

Here you see that the whole purpose of a Nazarite is someone who is separated unto the Lord. In our day, you can compare it to being a nun in a convent because they dress different. You can see that there is something different about their lives. In appearance today, some ministers wear collars, robes, or priestly garments and the minute you see them you know that this person is set apart for a religious calling or a divine appointment. This is what happened to the Nazarite if you saw someone, especially a male; he would have very long hair because they were not allowed to have razors touch their head. I am not sure of this, but I would imagine if they were not allowed to have a razor touch their head they wouldn't shave either, leaving them very long beards and mustaches.

Even now, Hasidic Jews have long hair on the side of their head because they do not cut their sideburns as a form of a Nazarite vow. Let us look at a couple of things that are obvious. The first is that a Nazarite could not drink any alcohol or fermented wine. They could not have grapes, raisins, or anything like that. In the Jewish custom of that time, they would have a glass of wine with dinner as we would have water. They did not get drunk; they would drink wine, as we would have a cup of coffee at the end of a meal. Even today in Italy, Christians have a glass of wine with dinner and are not convicted at all because they are not drunk with wine; it is their custom. Therefore, no Nazarite could have a drink for the entire time of their separation. The second thing as you saw earlier was they could not get their haircut. In addition, the third thing we see is that they could not touch a dead body, not even if their father collapsed dead on the ground, they could not hold their Dad. If they touched him, they would now become unclean and would have to go through all kinds of rituals. Therefore, they could not come near a dead body, no matter what. It does say in verse 9, *"if any men die very suddenly by him, and he hath defiled the head of his consecration; then he shall shave his head in the day of his cleansing, on the seventh day shall he shave it."* Further, on in the verses you will see all the rituals that they would have to go through in order to become clean once again.

The most famous Nazarite that we know of is Samson. According to Scripture, 'Samson lost his validity as a Nazarite long before Delilah ever cut his hair.' Samson married a Philistine woman. In some commentaries of the Bible, it says; that when Sampson made the covenant of marriage, he took some wine, and that this was the beginning of his downfall. The culture of that day was to toast at a wedding between the bride and groom of a Canaanite or Philistine wedding with wine. This is where Samson lost his first vow by drinking the wine at the wedding according to tradition of that day. Now I can show you for sure in Judges chapter 14, Sampson put his hand in the dead carcass of a lion to pull out some honey and broke his second vow. Then we know that he got his hair cut by Delilah and he lost his strength. One of the most frightening verses in the book of Judges is where it says that Sampson knew not that the Spirit of God had departed from him. You see that is what happens when we compromise in degrees, not with any big blatant sin; just a little here and a little there. The next thing you know we are not experiencing the presence and the power of God like we have been accustomed to.

If you sense something like that happening in your life, you need to stop and ask God if there is something that you have done or if there is something you need to correct. I do not know about you, but I do not want to live without the anointing. The Bible says that Jesus obeyed God in all things and that God gave him the Holy Spirit without measure. I love the Scripture in Acts chapter 5. People tend to ask me all the time, 'Why is your ministry so anointed?' My response is 'because I do my very best to obey him.'

Acts 5:32 *"and we are his witnesses of these things; and so is the Holy Ghost, whom God hath given to them that obey him."*

There is another Nazarite, a young man, who was birthed out of prayer and became one of the best prophets in the Old Testament. His name is Samuel. If you remember in 1 Samuel 1, *"Hannah cried out that if you give me a son, no razor will touch his head."* She consecrated him a Nazarite before he was born. The other famous Nazarite that we know of in the New Testament is John the Baptist. Do you remember when Mary came to Elizabeth and the baby leapt in her womb? God told Elizabeth at that time, that her son, John, was to abstain from all fermented drinks, this is why he lived the life of a Nazarite. What we need to get from this and say to ourselves is that I need to be separate and consecrate my life obediently unto God.

The one thing I used to like about our Catholic church as a young girl was that they used to pray and consecrate themselves for a season to God. The other thing I liked about being brought up Roman Catholic is that they honored Lent much more than other non-Catholic churches. This does not mean that as Christians we do not honor Christ, or keep Good Friday, or that we do not honor the things He went through. I really liked the fact that we had to give up something for the 40 days of Lent. There are some people who do the Daniel fast and eat vegetables. Anything you feel that you can do to consecrate yourself to God would be a good thing. Remember, a byproduct of love is devotion. Where there is devotion there is a heart to obey; and obedience is better than sacrifice.

The polishing of the sapphire meant that you were a Nazarite and wholly devoted to God. The sapphire is the color of heaven, clear and blue as the sky. Sapphire is the stone of Simeon. Simeon did not fare so well as his brothers, he had a problem. Let us see exactly what was pronounced over Simeon as we look at his story in Genesis chapter 49.

> Genesis 49:5-7 *"Simeon and Levi are brethren; instruments of cruelty are in their habitations. O my soul, come not thou into their secret; unto their assembly, mine honor, be not thou united: for in their anger they slew a man, and in their self-will they digged down a wall. Cursed be their anger, for it was fierce; and their wrath, for it was cruel: I will divide them in Jacob, and scatter them in Israel."*

One of the first things you see about Simeon is that he is not really that polished. What it says about Simeon and Levi in verse 5 is just awful. It says that they are *"instruments of cruelty."* Now what this is referring to is Genesis chapter 34. They have a sister by the name of Dinah, and she went in to see the women of the town who lived in that area. While in the land, Dinah meets a man named Shechem, son of Hamor the Hivite, prince of the country. When he saw her, he took her, lay with her and defiled her. In other words, he raped her.

Genesis 34:1-7 *"And Dinah the daughter of Leah, which she bare unto Jacob, went out to see the daughters of the land. And when Shechem the son of Hamor the Hivite, prince of the country, saw her, he took her, and lay with her, and defiled her. And his soul clave unto Dinah the daughter of Jacob, and he loved the damsel, and spoke kindly unto the damsel. And Shechem spoke unto his father Hamor, saying, Get me this damsel to wife. And Jacob heard that he had defiled Dinah his daughter: now his sons were with his cattle in the field: and Jacob held his peace until they were come. And Hamor the father of Shechem went out unto Jacob to commune with him. And the sons of Jacob came out of the field when they heard it: and the men were grieved, and they were very wroth, because he had wrought folly in Israel in lying with Jacob's daughter: which thing ought not to be done."*

Simeon and Levi decided to go to the men in the city and say *"listen; we will give you all of our beautiful Israeli women if all of your men agree to be circumcised."* The Bible says on the third day still being sore from their circumcised, Simeon and Levi killed every one of them. Therefore, that is the reference in Genesis 49 where it mentions that they were instruments of cruelty. They really did an awful thing. Because one man defiled their sister, they killed an entire group of innocent men.I guess they figured that they could not get to Hamor because he was the prince of the country. Do you notice the serious problem that Simeon and Levi have is anger. Actually, in verse 6 it says that they have self-will; what can be more frightening than that? In the King James Version of verse 6 it says *"for in their anger, they killed a man and in their self-will they digged down a wall."* Now verse 7 says *"Cursed be their anger, because it was fierce; and their wrath, for it is cruel: I will divide them in Jacob and scatter them."* The issue here is uncontrolled anger. One of the versions describes them as being weapons of anger and weapons of cruelty.

Here are a couple of facts that I have found out about this particular verse. God's Word is infallible. In Numbers chapter 26 verse 14, it speaks of the plague, and of them going through the wilderness. It says that 63% of them perished and they became the smallest tribe. When God says he is going to scatter you and divide you, He is not kidding. This is what God will do when we do not control our anger and get into self-will. The Word says that God *"resists the proud."* To me, anger and pride go hand-in-hand.

Someone who walks in humility will not kick the dog or kick the cat and have a temper tantrum. Therefore, pride and anger are closely related in my way of thinking. To me, anger is like a ticking time bomb that you cannot just go and dismantle, it is set to go off in due season. I do not know how to dismantle a bomb but if I can pull out the trigger or dismantle the timer little by little, I will be able to hinder the impact. It will not have that terrible explosion and hurt innocent people in the surrounding area. If I try to attack my anger all at one time, it will go off and everyone suffers.

I am not an angry person and not given to anger, however, my father had no control over his anger; it was rage. He never got angry or violent until he was drunk. At five years, old I was traumatized when I witnessed my dad severely beat my brother. He took his head, slammed it through the wallboard, and knocked my brother unconscious. His body lay at my feet. I thought my brother had died. I remember opening my mouth because I wanted to scream but not a sound came out of my mouth. In the background, I could hear my mother screaming. My Dad was out of control, my brother was being beat up, (and I am not talking about being disciplined). My whole family was out of control and in chaos.

For over 20 years, I could not deal with any type of conflict. If anyone raised their voice, every bone in my body would shake and tremble. I never expressed any type of anger, because I was afraid that I would be like my dad if I got mad. I thought I would really hurt somebody. I would never hit my kids. I remember one time as I was changing my daughter and she kept rolling over. I must have been having a bad day because I remember thinking that I could just grab her little leg and pull her back. I knew that at that point I could hurt my daughter, so I picked her up and I put her little naked body on the carpet. I left the room because I knew I had the potential to harm her. This might shock you, but when people have all this stuff going on and they are so messed up inside, sometimes the innocent suffer.

Then as I was in the process of my healing, and the Lord was helping me to recover, I began to look into the Scriptures. One day I realized I could express anger. I got angry with my husband. My way of dealing with anger was to get in the car, go to the mall and go shopping. When I came home, my husband asked me what was for dinner. I opened the freezer, took out a frozen chicken, and threw it in the sink. Then I said, 'Here's your dinner.' I chipped my sink and I have had to look at that chip in my sink every day since that event. Do not kid yourself and think you can never lose your temper or you can never get angry.

Look at what the Bible has to say about anger. Simeon's issue was wrath, violence, and anger. I want to tell you that in a small portion of Scripture there are three different Greek words for anger, they are *orgizo, parorgismos, and thymos.* Stay with me as I explain the meanings of each of these Greek words down for you.

If you look at Ephesians chapter 4 verse 26 *"be ye angry, and sin not: let not the sun go down upon your wrath."* That means there are times when we have righteous indignation and we have a right to be angry, without sinning. Here is an example: I am angry because abortions are allowed in America. I am angry that evil predators are molesting children. I believe that there is a good, wholesome anger from the Lord. As long as I do not decide to go out and kill every pedophile or blow up abortion clinics and kill doctors and nurses. Do you follow me? There is a place where you can be angry and not sin. Jesus got angry and did not sin, but we are not Jesus. Now let us continue in verse 26 and look at the word anger. In Greek, its translation is *orgizō* and it means, "to provoke, to arouse to anger." Isn't it true that when you know someone well you know how to provoke, arouse them, or how to anger them?

My husband knows exactly how to push my buttons, and I have learned how to push his. We can even do this with a smile. I realize that this does not make God happy. God does not want us to provoke one another and cause each other to get angry. The next portion of the Scripture says, *"not to let the sun go down upon your anger or wrath."* In Greek, wrath is *parorgismos* and it means "indignation and exasperation." What we must always remember is that verse 26 appears or comes before verse 27; we use verse 27 all the time, *"Neither give the devil any place."*

If the verse before says in your anger do not sin, the next verse says neither give the devil any place. Can you guess what gives place to the devil? Anger and evil speaking both do. When you get angry, you are going to say things that you should not and you will not be able to take them back.

> Ephesians 4:29, 31, 32 *"Let no corrupt communication proceed out of your mouth, but that which is good to the use of edifying, that it may minister grace unto the hearer. And grieve not the Holy Spirit of God, whereby ye are sealed unto the day of redemption. Let all bitterness, and wrath, and anger, and clamor, and evil speaking, be put away from you, with all malice: And be ye kind one to another, tenderhearted, forgiving one another, even as God for Christ's sake hath forgiven you."*

The only solution for anger is repentance, forgiveness, and kindness. Here is what I know. Even as I treat you is the way I will be treated. If I was angry with you and I stay mad at you, even after you have asked me to forgive you, that means I am keeping an arrogant attitude, staying mean hearted and nasty. God is going to resist me and He is not going to forgive me. So let us remember to be quick to forgive. Remember that Simeon's main problem was anger.

Let us look at the third Greek definition for wrath. In Greek, wrath is *thymos,* which means to "heat up and boil over." If you do not deal with the little issues, those little issues sit on the back burner and tend to get hotter and hotter. All of a sudden, you have boiled over. You know, nine times out of ten, the things that people are fighting about are not really the main issue. When you start bickering over little, simple things such as, the way a person drives, if you forget to put the cap back on the toothpaste, etc. it means for the most part something else is going on. I have decided in my life, with God's help, that as soon as I get angry, I will own it. I am not going to deny it. I am going to give it to God and repent. I go for hours sometimes and write or journal what I would really like to tell the person who I am angry with. Sometimes I break the point of my pencil so I have to use a pen, but after I am done writing it down, I rip it up, give it to God on the altar, repent, and throw it out. You have to do whatever it takes to defuse anger.

The tribes of Simeon were men of war. Why, because they had an angry leader; look at the past revolutions and revolts. There is usually someone in leadership who is pounding their fist and leading the charge. It is contagious; all of a sudden, they are all going out there and they do not know what they are mad about in the first place. The Book of Numbers shows us where God called every single male from the age of twenty and up to go to war.

> Numbers 1:22-23 *"Of the children of Simeon, by their generations, after their families, by the house of their fathers, those that were numbered of them, according to the number of the names, by their polls, every male from twenty years old and upward, all that were able to go forth to war; Those that were numbered of them, even of the tribe of Simeon, were fifty and nine thousand and three hundred."*

Please understand that you are not alone concerning this issue of anger. Just to name a few individuals who had issues with anger; Naaman in the Old Testament comes to mind and James and John in the New Testament come to mind. James and John, the sons of Zebedee, wanted to call down fire from heaven and burn up a whole village.

I was reading a book recently and it said that Jesus told James and John that He was going to call them the Sons of Thunder. He was no longer going to call them the Sons of Zebedee, because they were so easily angered. Yet, years later, when John penned the book of 1 John, the love of God had so changed him that he was not angry anymore. He even ministered to the people he wanted to kill. In Luke chapter 9, when Jesus wanted to go into Samaria, the people of the village did not want to receive Him. James and John got so angry that they said to Jesus, *"Let's call down fire and let's burn them all up."* Jesus responded by saying, *"You don't know what spirit you are of."*

Let me warn you that unbridled anger if you do not repent of and turn from will become a spirit of anger. Years later, in the Book of Acts, you see that when Samaria received the Word of God, they called on James and John to lay hands on them so that they would receive the gift of the Holy Spirit. There is hope for all of us because God changes lives. The very men who wanted to call down fire and burn them up are now extending a hand to heal them and impart the gifts of the Holy Spirit to them. Thank God for change!

> Judges 1:1-3 *"Now after the death of Joshua it came to pass, that the children of Israel asked the LORD, saying, who shall go up for us against the Canaanites first, to fight against them? And the LORD said Judah shall*

*go up: behold, I have delivered the land into his hand. And Judah said unto Simeon his brother, come up with me into my lot, that we may fight against the Canaanites; and I likewise will go with thee into thy lot. So Simeon went with him."*

Therefore, you see in the first two verses here that they are called to war. In the third verse, we see that they are fighting men. Finally, look at Judges 1:17, *"And Judah went with Simeon his brother, and they slew the Canaanites that inhabited Zephath, and utterly destroyed it. And the name of the city was called Hormah."*

They destroyed the Canaanites that inhabited Zephath and renamed the city. The name of the city is *Hormah,* which means "devotion." Remember the definition for a *Nazarite* is, "devoted to the Lord." How interesting it is that Simeon was used to devote a city to God, since his stone the *sapphire* is "to polish" as one who devotes himself to God.

## Key Point

The Second Row of Stones
- ◆ Stone One: The Emerald of Reuben
  - – The emerald represents the throne for all of us who are the firstborn of many brethren
- ◆Stone Two: Sapphire of Simeon:
  - – We are polished for victory in war because we are devoted to God

## Closing Prayer

*Father, I just want to thank You, Lord. I love your Word. God, I know that this has been an unusual thing to study and yet, Lord, I am a Nazarite. I have taken that vow of separation unto You. You said, "Come out and be ye separate and don't touch the unclean thing." Lord, I am devoted to You and I am consecrated to You. Lord, I ask You to help me, when I get angry, not to sin. Help me not to let the sun go down on my wrath lest I give the devil place. Lord, Your Word tells me about the Tribe of Simeon; and even though they were men of war, and had victory. They ended up being devoted to the things of your kingdom, yet the man Simeon himself had some cruelty, violence, and wrath in him. Lord, I do not want any of those characteristics in me. Therefore, as a sapphire, Lord, I ask You to polish me. I ask You to put Your hand heavy upon me and begin to grind that stone until I am a beautiful, clear blue; something that shows the Glory of God as seen in the book of Exodus. There it says, "That they saw God and in His presence His pathway was polished like sapphire." In closing Lord, help me as a Nazarite, who has taken a vow to serve you, to love you, and to be devoted to you all the days of my life. Help me to get anger out of my life so that I may be kind, tenderhearted, and merciful to others, even as You have been so kind, tender, forgiving, and merciful to me. I ask Your blessing upon this word. In Jesus Name, Amen.*

# CHAPTER 7

## – The Sixth Stone –
## The Diamond of Gad

*Father, I would just like to thank You that everything we need for life is given to us through the knowledge of the Scriptures. I ask that we would have more insight, wisdom, revelation, and knowledge Your Word. Father, we want to put Your Word into practice in our everyday life. Thank You for all that You are showing us through the stones of the breastplate of the high priest. Thank You that in the book of Peter, You call us living stones, a royal priesthood to show forth the praises of Him who calls us out of darkness into His marvelous light. We just want to thank You for what we are about to learn and glean from the Word of God. We thank You for the Holy Spirit, who will lead and guide us into the truth of your Word, in Jesus Name. Amen.*

In this chapter, we are going to cover the last stone of the second row of the breastplate of the high priest. What we are going to learn in this chapter is astounding. We are going to study the diamond of Gad. I would like to introduce you to the tribe of Gad. The Key Definition for *Gad* which is "a troop cometh" is found in the verse below. His stone is the diamond. The Key Definition for the word *diamond* is "to break in pieces by bruising."

Genesis 30:11. *"And Leah said, A troop cometh: and she called his name Gad. "*

As you continue to read this chapter, you will see what this troop does and how amazing the prophecy and blessing from his father, Jacob, and his spiritual father, Moses, can be. You will understand what this troop of Gad had to bruise and overcome. From my understanding of gemstones, there are certain precious stones that cannot be placed in any harsh chemicals. I know that my Onyx and my Ruby ring have to be placed in a less caustic solution, but my diamond can be placed in any type of chemical and it will not hurt it at all. In addition, a good diamond can actually cut glass; which is how one can tell if it is a fake diamond or the real diamond.

> Jeremiah 17:1 *"The sin of Judah is written with a pen of iron, and with the point of a diamond: it is graven upon the table of their heart, and upon the horns of your altars;"*

I know that I am pulling the following Scripture out of its actual setting, but there is something of interest about the diamond found in the book of Jeremiah. Evidently, if you just look at this verse, it says that a diamond is actually used to engrave. The point of a diamond is sharp enough to engrave. In other words, it is as sharp as a pen of iron.

In Genesis 49 we will look at the blessing of Jacob over his son Gad. We are going to look at several different versions of the Bible for this Scripture, as the King James Version does not do it justice.

> (KJV) Genesis 49:19 *"Gad, a troop shall overcome him: but he shall overcome at the last."*

> (NIV) Genesis 49:19 *"And Gad will be attacked by a band of raiders, but he will attack them at their heels."*

> (Amplified) Genesis 49:19 *"Gad, a raiding troop shall raid him, but he shall raid at their heels and assault them [victoriously]."*

This is a short verse but it is packed with truth. Therefore, what comes from Gad is a troop that overcomes in the end. They do not always get victory in the beginning, but in the end, they always overcome. Here are some different translations of the Bible so we can study this Scripture further.

Did you notice that the King James is the only version that does not mention Gad bruising or attacking the heel? Therefore, we find that Gad is a troop that overcomes in the end and attacks the enemy at their heel.

What this means literally is, that he will trip them up and cause them to fall. If you grab me by my heel, I am going down. If someone were to grab you by your heel, you would be unable to catch your balance and you would fall. Even though Gad does not start well, he is victorious in the end. The fact that he grabs them by his heel leads me to the Book of Genesis.

This is one of the very first promises found in the book of Genesis concerning the coming of the Messiah. The Scripture says something about Jesus that I think we need to look at. It is in Genesis chapter 3; it is after the woman and her husband sinned and ate from the forbidden fruit.

> Genesis 3:14 *"And the LORD God said unto the serpent, Because thou hast done this, thou art cursed above all cattle, and above every beast of the field; upon thy belly shalt thou go, and dust shalt thou eat all the days of thy life."*

Reading verse 14 you realize that serpents must have walked, because now their curse was to move on their bellies. Frankly, I cannot imagine a snake walking into a room. The verse says, 'you are cursed.' Unfortunately, for us, the serpent's main path is the dust of the earth. You know that the Bible says that 'God made man from the dust of the earth.' We who are dust of the earth have become the main course for the serpent.

> Isaiah 65:25 *"the serpent's food is the dust of man or the dust of the earth."*

Thank God that in Genesis chapter 3 we have a promise of the coming Messiah who will defeat the serpent. In the verse below, you see that God will put hate or enmity between the serpent and the woman. It is no wonder there are more women who are afraid of snakes than men. Most women have an inbred hatred or loathing of snakes. I do not know of many women who have snakes for pets. However, there are some men who have Boa constrictors for pets; they keep on getting larger and larger glass enclosures for them to live in, and they keep on feeding them. I cannot imagine throwing a rat into a glass enclosure and watching an animal devour its pray.

> Genesis 3:15 *"And I will put enmity between thee and the woman, and between thy seed and her seed; it shall bruise thy head, and thou shalt bruise his heel."*

God said he was going to put hatred between the serpent and the woman, now watch this: *"And I will put enmity between thee and the woman, and between thy seed and her seed."* When a woman ovulates, she has the potential to have a child she passes an egg. Ovulation is the most fertile period of a woman's cycle. When a woman and her husband are intimate, his seed meets her egg and conception takes place. It is so interesting, because women are not seed bearing. God said to Eve, *"your seed is going to bruise the heel of the enemy."* This verse is talking about Jesus being the seed and it says in verse 15 *"between thy seed and her seed, it shall bruise thy head, and thou shalt bruise his heel."* Therefore, without getting too complex, the first prophecy about Christ's coming was that He was going to bruise the serpent's heel. Because of Jesus Christ being the seed of the woman, we can also bruise the enemy.

When you look at the tribe of Gad you understand that *Gad* is a troop that overcomes in the end. The way he overcomes is that he has a diamond, and the diamond is the stone that needs to bruise the heel. In all of this, we, like Gad, can overcome. I would like to overcome in the beginning how about you? I would even be happy to overcome in the middle. Nevertheless, sometimes you have to go through and overcome at the end. The promise is that Gad will overcome and will bruise the heel of the enemy.

Now let us go over some Scriptures on how we overcome, and then we are going to spend a bit of time looking at what Moses had to say about Gad. I want to show you an awesome Scripture in the book of Revelation, which describes how we, like a troop, overcome in the end.

Revelation 12:9-11 *"And the great dragon was cast out, that old serpent, called the devil, and Satan, which deceives the whole world: he was cast out into the earth, and his angels were cast out with him. And I heard a loud voice saying in heaven, Now is come salvation, and strength, and the kingdom of our God, and the power of his Christ: for the accuser of our brethren is cast down, which accused them before our God day and night. And they overcame him by the Blood of the Lamb and by the word of their testimony; and they loved not their lives unto the death."*

Notice how in verse 9 the enemy has four names: the great dragon, the old serpent, the Devil, and Satan; it speaks of his device of deception. Aren't you glad that we have the truth in us and we do not have to be deceived by the tricks and the lies of the enemy? In verse 10, please notice that Satan's mode of operation is that he is the accuser of brethren. He is going to accuse you before God and before men. You see that in verse 11 they overcame him by the Blood of the Lamb and the word of their testimony. It goes on to say, having not loved their life to the end. Never forget that the way you and I overcome is by the Blood of the Lamb. The minute you and I think we are a match for the enemy and that we can overcome all the works of the enemy by ourselves, we are in for a severe fall. He has had 6000 years or more to practice his art of deception. Satan is the father of lies. He knows exactly how to deceive you and how to push your buttons.

What affects me might not affect you he surely knows what he is doing. I have heard some people say that they pulled the teeth out of that slew foot (the devil). I am not going to talk like that. I'm not afraid of him because I fear God, but I have enough respect to know that without the anointing of the Holy Spirit and without the Blood of the Lamb I am no match for an unclean, fallen angel who still has quite a bit of power. Do not underestimate the enemy. The way to overcome him is by the Blood of the Lamb and the word of your testimony.

We really do not want any challenges. Let us be honest here. We want things to be easy and full of enjoyment as well as to be highly favored, and overtaken by good things. However, you know, you cannot celebrate a victory unless you have had a battle. Until we go through some things, we will never know what it is to overcome. The Bible says that *Gad*, like all of us, is a troop of overcomers. The way they overcame at the end and the way we overcome, is through the seed, Jesus, bruising the heel of the enemy, using that diamond that grabs him by the heel.

Romans 8:35-37 *"Who shall separate us from the love of Christ? shall tribulation, or distress, or persecution, or famine, or nakedness, or peril, or sword? As it is written, for thy sake we are killed all the daylong; we are accounted as sheep for the slaughter. Nay, in all these things we are more than conquerors through him that loved us."*

Can I tell you in all honesty; when I read verse 35, I realized that very few of us have experienced this. Not many of us really understand what it is to go through persecution and famine. Our idea of poverty is having the cable turned off while still having two cars in the driveway. You will never understand what this is until you experience it. I saw famine in India that was unimaginable. People go for months with just a bag of rice. There was so much malnutrition, devastation, sickness, and disease. Our country really does not know what it means to be in a famine.

In verse 36, it says, *"for thy sake we are killed all the day long."* You have to understand that when Paul wrote this, they were persecuting and killing Christians. As a matter-of-fact, when they killed James they all rejoiced and decided they would imprison Peter. Can you imagine that? They killed James with a sword and the people were so happy after they killed James that they got Peter and put him in prison. Praise God for the Angel that freed him. So let us continue in verse 36, *"and we are counted as sheep for the slaughter."*

*Look at verse 37 in this context, "We are more than conquerors through him that loved us."* We are not just conquerors because we are more than conquerors. A conqueror is someone who goes into battle, defeats the enemy, and brings back the victory. I am more than a conqueror and I did not have to fight for it. This is what Jesus did for you and me. Let me encourage you, like *Gad*, we will overcome in the end. If you are going through something right now, you cannot go around it, but be encouraged and know that in the end you will overcome. Never forget the Blood of the Lamb and the word of your testimony.

I want to paint the best picture that I possibly can of what Gad represents through Moses blessing. What is it to have the victory, and to be as sharp as a diamond that can actually engrave, cut and bruise the enemy? See what Moses has to say about Gad in Deuteronomy. The Bible tells us here that Gad dwells as a lion. I believe it is essential that we get a good picture of the lion, the king of the forest. I am going to take you through several Scriptures and we are going to glean something different from everyone. If you want to overcome in the end, you have to have the heart of a lion. Otherwise, you are going to become prey for the enemy.

Deuteronomy 33:20 *"And of Gad he said, blessed be he that enlarged Gad: he dwelleth as a lion, and teareth the arm with the crown of the head."*

Do you see where is states that the word of God says that in order to overcome we must be like a lion.

1 Peter 5:8 *"Be sober, be vigilant; because your adversary the devil, as a roaring lion, walketh about, seeking whom he may devour:"*

I have heard this Scripture misquoted often. The Bible does not say that Satan is a lion. It says he goes around "as a roaring lion." There is a difference between being a lion and going around as a lion. Remember, the Bible says that Satan's ministers come as angels of light. Let us not forget that there is only one lion and He is the Lion of the Tribe of Judah. His name is Jesus and He has completely overcome and has bruised the head of the enemy once and for all.

In the book of Revelation, it says that Jesus is the one who wears *"the many crowns."* It speaks of Him riding a white horse, and all the armies of the children of God were riding with Him. Throughout the Scripture, there are many references to crowns. In the book of Revelation, it is written that 'we will cast our crowns at His feet.' Gad overcomes by bruising the heel of the enemy but he also overcomes with a crown on his head. Therefore, the way we overcome is to understand that Jesus is the King of Kings and Lord of Lords and on his head are many crowns. There are many different crowns, for instance, there is the crown of a soul winner. Whenever you bring someone to the Lord there is a crown that is given to you as a reward. As an evangelist, can you imagine how many crowns Billy Graham will be given? The crowns he has won would be enough to fill a room. If there were a crown for every man or woman you have lead to the Lord, how many would there be? In Billy Graham's crusades, there are thousands and thousands of people who have come to the Lord. What a blessing to lay so many crowns at the feet of his Savior.

Here are five the crowns that are mentioned in the Scriptures: The Crown of Glory for the faithful servant, which is found in 1 Peter 5:4. The Crown of Rejoicing for soul winners, which is referenced in 1 Thessalonians 2:19. The Crown of Righteousness for those who love His return is referenced in 2 Timothy 4:8. The Imperishable Crown, is the fourth crown and is found in 1Corinthians 9:25. Finally, the fifth crown in Revelation 2:10 is the Crown of Life given to Christian martyrs.

(KJV) 2 Samuel 17:10 *"And he also that is valiant, whose heart is as the heart of a lion, shall utterly melt: for all Israel knoweth that thy father is a mighty man, and they which be with him are valiant men."*

(Amplified) 2 Samuel 17:10 *"And even he who is brave, whose heart is as the heart of a lion, will utterly melt, for all Israel knows that your father is a mighty man and that those who are with him are brave men."*

(NIV) 2 Samuel 17:10 *"Then even the bravest soldier, whose heart is like the heart of a lion, will melt with fear, for all Israel knows that your father is a fighter and that those with him are brave."*

Here in verse 10, first you notice that you should have the heart of a lion. The next word you should notice is valiant. In the Hebrew transliteration it is *'chayil,'* which means "strength, power, might (especially warlike) valor, or to show one's self as strong in valor." In the Amplified and NIV versions, the word brave or bravest is used. The definition from the Merriam-Webster dictionary for *brave* or *bravest* is, "having or showing courage [a brave soldier]." In order for us to overcome in this life, we have to be brave and have courage. Therefore, we recognize that the heart of a lion is brave. I have never seen a lion shake or cower in fear. The heart of a lion is brave.

1 Chronicles 12:8 *"And of the Gadites there separated themselves unto David into the hold to the wilderness men of might, and men of war fit for the battle, that could handle shield and buckler, whose faces were like the faces of lions,"*

Can you see how this is quite a verse? If you want to overcome like Jesus, this is the attitude that you have to have. First, we see that the Gadites separated themselves. We have to be separate and not touch unclean things if we are really going to have victory. Not only did they separate themselves but also they were men of might and men of war. They were fit for battle and could handle their weapons. Their faces were like the faces of lions.

A lion is ready for any fight that comes along. The Gadites knew how to handle their weapons. Do you know how to handle your weapons of warfare? We have the sword of the Spirit and the Word of God. Did you know that praise is also a weapon that silences the enemy? We have to know how and when to say, *"It is written."* So far here is what have we established;

Gad is a lion who gets victory with a crown on his head. He has the heart of a lion, which means he is very brave. He is not afraid of the battle and he is ready for war. He knows how and when to use his weapons and remains ready to fight.

Job 10:16 *"For it increaseth. Thou huntest me as a fierce lion: and again thou shewest thyself marvelous upon me."*

When the lion is stalking its prey, the lion changes its posture by lowering its head and body, staying low to the ground while keeping focused on its prey. When the prey looks vulnerable, the lion creeps closer. If the prey becomes startled, the lion will cease its movement and remain still until it is the right time to strike. After the lion has entered into striking distance, it pounces, and the chase ends with the prey's demise.

Remember you are to be as Gad; brave and ready to fight with a heart of a lion. You have to know how to fight, you have to know how to use your weapons, and you have to be as fierce as a lion. You cannot be wimpy and make some kind of weak declaration. You have to be bold, strong men and women of God. The Lord thy God is with you and you should never be afraid to say, *"in the Name of the Jesus, I come against you, by the Blood of the Lamb and the word of my testimony. It is written..."*

Proverbs 28:1 *"The wicked flee when no man pursueth: but the righteous are bold as a lion."*

It is time that the body of Christ rises in boldness as a lion. This is what Gad does, they overcame because they have bravery, their men of war are fierce hunters, and they are bold. I am tired of all these cults enlisting people. They are not ashamed to talk to anyone, anywhere; like at the mall, in the elevator, or on the street. Here we are with the truth that sets men and women free, yet we are timid and shy. We need to pray for boldness of the Spirit. We need to stand strong in courage and say, "Lord, whatever You want me to fight against, I will." The Lord promised us victory in the end, and we shall overcome. The Lord wants us to have a bold spirit. It says, *"But the righteous are as bold as a lion."* Are you righteous? Sure, you are in Christ! You are because He gave us the gift of righteousness. So be bold as a lion!

Proverbs 30:30 *"A lion which is strongest among beasts, and turneth not away for any."*

Do you see that the lion is the strongest beast and, in essence, runs from nothing? On a scale of 1 to 10, if I were to ask you how you are doing in your lion attributes, what would you say? Are you bold and mighty? How victorious are you? How well do you use your weapons of warfare? The more you get this Word in you, the stronger you can be in God. If He wants me to be like a lion then that is what I want to be. I want to be brave and bold when I use my weapons; I want a victorious life in Christ. I want to win. I do not know of anyone who would go into a fight and want to lose.

There was a boy in my life by the name of Skipper. I think that Skipper liked me a little bit. He always used to pick on me and sometimes made fun of me. He also flirted with me a little bit. Well, one day Skipper went too far and he threw an ice ball at me. The ice ball hit me right in my temple and I lost it! I started to beat Skipper up, for lack of a better description, I was like a Tasmanian devil. I fought dirty, I fought mean and I fought hard. I grabbed Skipper and I pulled him by his ears and banged his head against the parked car. Then I stepped on his foot and started kicking him. I was spitting, biting, and scratching. He had blood running down his neck. His mother came running down the street screaming and had to pull me off him. Obviously, I did not date Skipper after that. I really was so angry that I did anything I could to win.

Years and years went by and I never saw Skipper again. Let us fast-forward thirty years. Here we are in Pleasantville New Jersey, where we have established this beautiful church. All of the pastors in the region along with our church decided to have a one year memorial service for all the family and service members that were lost in the 9/11 attacks. We did a beautiful presentation with PowerPoint and we invited the fire department, the paramedics, the EMTs, and the police to come in uniform. It was our way to say thank you from our community for all that they had done for us. I will never forget this for as long as I live. In marched the firefighters, the paramedics, the EMTs and finally the police came in. Well, do you want to know who the chief of police was at that time in our beautiful city? It was Skipper! All of a sudden, I realized that I did not just beat up anyone; I beat up the chief of police. I thought to myself, he is not going to recognize me. He walks in, comes up the steps, unhooks his holster, puts his hand on his pistol, and says, "Gwen, I owe you one." We both rolled in laughter. Now you and I know that you are not supposed to fight as a Christian, but if I have to fight, you know I am going to win. I am not going to get beat up. Listen, when Mike Tyson bit Evander Holyfield's ear off in the ring, I understand that, I would have bit his nose off! I can tell you that there is something that happens to a person when they become engaged and enraged when the heat of a battle.

The bottom line is that you have to have the mindset that you are going to win. I do not care how many times you are knocked down, and I do not care how many times you are tripped up. You have to keep getting up. When life kicks you to the curb, you have to get up. Because I have chosen to serve the Lord, I have won far more victories than I have lost. Now, I have lost a few, but I have won the majority because his Word says that I will overcome, and so will you. Let us be strong like the lion.

Isaiah 31:4 *"For thus hath the LORD spoken unto me, Like as the lion and the young lion roaring on his prey, when a multitude of shepherds is called forth against him, he will not be afraid of their voice, nor abase himself for the noise of them: so shall the LORD of hosts come down to fight for mount Zion, and for the hill thereof."*

In essence, Isaiah is saying that the lion is afraid of no one and its roar is fearless. Did you know that a lion does not roar until he has captured his prey? If the lion roars before he captures his prey, there is a good chance that his prey will get away. A lion has to be subtle, sneaky, and crouch down. He has to lie in wait for the weakest animal and when he grabs the animal by the neck, it is all over, down they go. Once they have defeated their prey they roar as if saying, "I'm all that." You do not roar ahead of time because you do not want to give the enemy any warning. You wait and when everyone should know you are victorious then you can give a shout. It is said that the roar of an adult lion and can be heard for up to 5 miles away.

Joel 1:6 *"For a nation is come up upon my land, strong, and without number, whose teeth are the teeth of a lion, and he hath the cheek teeth of a great lion."*

The lion has a strong jaw, with long canine teeth that are wide enough to fit between the neck bone and sever the spinal cord of even large prey. However, lions suffocate their prey with a bite to the muzzle or throat. They have modified molars, which are carnassials. These molars cut flesh with scissor-like precision; they do not waste a bite.

Let me review what we have covered in this chapter. The stone of Gad is a diamond. A diamond breaks in pieces and bruises. How does Gad overcome? They bruised the enemies' heels, through Christ Jesus. Deuteronomy states that the Gadites, the tribe of Gad, are like lions. I want to instill in you that you have to have the boldness of a lion with a lion type spirit. Just get it into your spirit that Jesus is the Lion of the Tribe of Judah. He has the victory with a crown on His head. We are going to ride with Him and behind Him as victors, so we might as well have the victory now. That is what Jesus won for us.

## Row One

The Sardius: Judah

- ◆ Because of the blood of Jesus, we can give praise to God

The Topaz: Issachar

- ◆ You are rewarded for service

The Carbuncle: Zebulun

- ◆ We dwell in the light

## Row Two

The Emerald: Ruben

- ◆ The throne of the firstborn will see Jesus;
  this is the covenant of promise

The Sapphire: Simeon

- ◆ God has heard me and he is polishing me
  through affliction

The Diamond: Gad

- ◆ We are more than conquerors through the Crown of Jesus,
  the Great Lion who bruised Satan

## Closing Prayer

*Father, thank You for these first two rows of living stones; I ask that You continue to minister to me and help me to recall what You are saying to me throughout this book. You have reminded me that I am a troop, and like the Gadites, I am an overcomer. I overcome by the Blood of the Lamb and the word of my testimony. I ask You to make me bold as a lion, to help me to be unafraid and to be fierce in my attack as I overcome. I thank you that as I ride with You I have victory. I pray one day I will cast or lay down all my crowns at Your feet. I praise You as the Lion of Judah my conquering King. In Jesus Name. Amen.*

# CHAPTER 8

# – The Seventh Stone –
# The Ligure of Ephraim

*Father, we come to You with thankful hearts for Your awesome Word. And we know that Your Word is settled in heaven. And Father, as we begin to look at the third row of stones in the breastplate of the high priest help each one of us to remember that we are not doing this just to gain knowledge. We are here to implement the truth you show us into our lives because we are a royal priesthood, and we are living stones. Father, we ask that the Holy Spirit would make this word real to us while helping us to implement it in our lives. In Jesus Name. Amen.*

In this chapter we will cover information on the first stone in the third row of the breastplate. For some reason, the next two tribes on the breastplate are not from the original sons of Jacob. The first stone in the third row is the ligure of Ephraim and then in chapter nine we will see that the second stone in the third row is an agate of Manasseh.

Ephraim and Manasseh were not Jacob's sons; they are the two sons of Joseph. There were two tribes or sons of Jacob that were not included into the breastplate. They were the tribe of Levi and the tribe of Joseph. A question you might have is how Joseph was not included on the breastplate since he was Jacobs' favorite son. I believe I have come up with the information to answer to this question. The reason, I believe is because Levi is the priesthood and Joseph is a type of Christ.

In the Old Testament, the life of Joseph parallels the life of Jesus. He was the favorite son, born of a miracle, sold into slavery, deceived by his brothers, and all of the things that happened to Joseph happened to Jesus as well. The one thing I am positively sure of is what the tribe of Ephraim represents. I know how to tie what the stone represents together and it is exhilarating.

> Genesis 41:42-52  *"And Pharaoh took off his ring from his hand, and put it upon Joseph's hand, and arrayed him in vestures of fine linen, and put a gold chain about his neck; And he made him to ride in the second chariot which he had; and they cried before him, Bow the knee: and he made him ruler over all the land of Egypt. Moreover, Pharaoh said unto Joseph, I am Pharaoh, and without thee shall no man lift up his hand or foot in all the land of Egypt. In addition, Pharaoh called Joseph's name Zaphnathpaaneah; and he gave him to wife Asenath the daughter of Potipherah priest of On. Moreover, Joseph went out over all the land of Egypt. Joseph was thirty years old when he stood before Pharaoh King of Egypt. Joseph went out from the presence of Pharaoh, and went throughout all the land of Egypt. In the seven plenteous years, the earth brought forth by handfuls. In addition, he gathered up all the food of the seven years, which were in the land of Egypt, and laid up the food in the cities: the food of the field, which was round about every city; Joseph gathered corn as the sand of the sea, very much, until he left numbering; for it was without number. In addition, unto Joseph were born two sons before the years of famine came, which Asenath the daughter of Potipherah priest of On bare unto him. Joseph called the name of the firstborn Manasseh: For God, said he, hath made me forget all my toil, and my entire father's house. And the name of the second called he Ephraim: For God hath caused me to be fruitful in the land of my affliction."*

The story of Joseph is found in the book of Genesis. The story starts in chapter 37 and ends in chapter 50. The narrative of Joseph is one of the longest in the Bible. As you read above you can see that Joseph's life was one of forgiveness and reconciliation. Throughout his life, he was able to find favor in the midst of tribulation; even during the time he was incarcerated. Joseph ends up becoming second in power of a Nation; second only to Pharaoh, Egypt's ruler. Joseph is also given a woman to marry Asenath she was the daughter of Potipherah the priest of On.

Together they had two sons Manasseh and Ephraim. Did you notice that Ephraim was the second son born. Make a mental note that you will learn more about Manasseh in chapter nine; however, you must understand the meaning behind both of these sons' names. This way you will know why Ephraim ends up first on the breastplate even though he was not the first-born son.

The Key Definition for *Manasseh* is, "God has caused me to forget or God has helped me to forget my past." If there is anything we need to bare in our lives, it is a Manasseh spirit. With a spirit of Manasseh no matter where we have been or what we have gone through in our lives, God has a future for us and we cannot keep living in the past or living in regret of our mistakes. We need to move forward and know that he has plans to prosper us and not to harm us. This is why I believe that Joseph names his first son Manasseh, 'because with his birth he wanted God to please help him forget his past.' If I had been walking in the shoes of Joseph, I would have named my first-born, 'revenge' and my second born, 'I told you so' and on and on the list of names would go. However, whenever adversity came, Joseph responded with faith, hope, and confidence in God. In verse 52, Joseph names his second son Ephraim "God has caused me to be fruit-ful in the land of my affliction."

The Key Definition for *Ephraim* is "fruitful in affliction" or, in essence, "to receive double for any trouble you've had in your life."

You know, if I ever were to conceive two sons spiritually, I would have wanted to birth both of these two boys. I would like to be able to say, 'God has helped me to forget my past.' Not only that but 'He's made me doubly fruitful for everything the enemy has tried to do to me.'

Ephraim's stone is the ligure. This stone is a very hard stone to describe. I have spent hours doing research to figure out the meaning of this stone and what it looks like. One of the most important things for us to remember is that it is not about what the stone looks like but what it means. The Key Definition for *ligure* is "to engrave a seal." The ligure stone is a sky blue in color.

Let me show you how God wants to give us double blessings and how we have been engraved and sealed. Earlier I asked you to notice that Manasseh is the first-born and that Ephraim is the second born to Joseph. I want you to see in Genesis chapter 48 where Jacob is about to die and bestows the blessings on his two grandsons.

> Genesis 48:13-20 *"And Joseph took them both, Ephraim in his right hand toward Israel's left hand, and Manasseh in his left hand toward Israel's right hand, and brought them near unto him. And Israel stretched out his right hand, and laid it upon Ephraim's head, who was the younger, and his left hand upon Manasseh's head, guiding his hands wittingly; for Manasseh was the firstborn. And he blessed Joseph, and said, God, before whom my father's Abraham and Isaac did walk, the God which fed me all my life long unto this day, The Angel which redeemed me from all evil, bless the lads; and let my name be named on them, and the name of my father's Abraham and Isaac; and let them grow into a multitude in the midst of the earth. And when Joseph saw that his father laid his right hand upon the head of Ephraim, it displeased him: and he held up his father's hand, to remove it from Ephraim's head unto Manasseh's head. And Joseph said unto his father, Not so, my father: for this is the firstborn; put thy right hand upon his head. And his father refused, and said, I know it, my son, I know it: he also shall become a people, and he also shall be great: but truly his younger brother shall be greater than he, and his seed shall become a multitude of nations. And he blessed them that day, saying, In thee shall Israel bless, saying, God make thee as Ephraim and as Manasseh: and he set Ephraim before Manasseh. And Israel said unto Joseph, Behold, I die: but God shall be with you, and bring you again unto the land of your fathers. Moreover, I have given to thee one portion above thy brethren, which I took out of the hand of the Amorite with my sword and with my bow."*

This chapter probably was the one that showed when they were placed into the heart of Jacob and were added into the lineage as well as on the breastplate. Whether we are a Manasseh or an Ephraim God wants us to be fruitful in our afflictions, and to forget the pain of our past. Jesus is the firstborn of many brothers. Because of Jesus, we too have the right to become the sons and daughters of God. Therefore, we now have been given the right to be included in the line of Jesus; we have now been grafted into the vine.

We are going to look at four scriptures that show us what happens when someone steals your blessing. There are three verses I want to show you that all talk about how we have a right to claim twice as much when something has been stolen from us. They are found in Exodus chapter 22 verses 4 and 7, then finally in verse 9.

> Exodus 22:1-9 *"If a man shall steal an ox, or a sheep, and kill it, or sell it; he shall restore five oxen for an ox, and four sheep for a sheep. If a thief be found breaking up, and be smitten that he die, there shall no blood be shed for him. If the sun be risen upon him, there shall be bloodshed for him; for he should make full restitution; if he have nothing, then he shall be sold for his theft. If the theft be certainly found in his hand alive, whether it be ox, or ass, or sheep; he shall restore double. If a man shall cause a field or vineyard to be eaten, and shall put in his beast, and shall feed in another man's field; of the best of his own field, and of the best of his own vineyard, shall he make restitution. If fire break out, and catch in thorns, so that the stacks of corn, or the standing corn, or the field, be consumed therewith; he that kindled the fire shall surely make restitution. If a man shall deliver, unto his neighbor's money or stuff to keep, and it be stolen out of the man's house; if the thief be found, let him pay double. If the thief be not found, then the master of the house shall be brought unto the judges, to see whether he have put his hand unto his neighbor's goods. For all manner of trespass, whether it be for ox, for ass, for sheep, for raiment, or for any manner of lost thing which another challenges to be his, the cause of both parties shall come before the judges; and whom the judges shall condemn, he shall pay double unto his neighbors."*

Did you see that in verse four it states 'that if something is stolen they must restore or return double to you?' The apostle John points out to us in his book, in chapter 10 verse 10 that the 'thief comes to steal, kill, and destroy us.' Yet, if you continue reading this verse, you would see where it shows us the following, 'He comes so you might have life and that it would be more abundantly.' Look below for yourself do you see what it says? John clearly states that 'Satan is a thief and a robber,' so would God want to take our blessings away from us? Absolutely not! God to 'bless us exceedingly abundantly' above all we can ask or think for, according to the power that works in us.

> John 10:10 *"The thief cometh not, but for to steal, and to kill, and to destroy: I am come that they might have life, and that they might have it more abundantly."*

Remember this, that when you are in the land of affliction as Joseph was for a long time; it isn't God who is withholding the blessing or the one punishing you. It is the enemy as he is the one who comes to rob, kill, and destroy us. In addition, Jesus calls the enemy a thief. So I thought if the enemy is a thief, what happens when the thief is found out? He has to restore a double blessing. He has to give back twice as much as was stolen.

Jesus came to take back everything that the enemy first took from us in the garden. In the Exodus chapter 22 verse 7, it states that 'when something is stolen from your house, the thief has to pay back double.' Here is another affirmation to us that when the enemy tries to steal from us and he becomes found out, he has to pay back double.

Let me show you again in this same chapter where in verse 9, it speaks of all manners of trespass. Once again, we see that 'we will have to be paid back double, and it has to be something that he has stolen from you.' It cannot be something that you abused, or you did not appreciate. Did you see during your reading about Joseph that gets more than double for all that he went through? Because of his attitude in the land of affliction, he names his firstborn son, 'only to forget the pain from my past' and names his second son, 'There is a reason for this affliction and God wants to give me a double blessing.' Praise the Lord that as we walk through our affliction God wants to give us a double blessing.

I think that sometimes we are too 'enemy conscious' and not enough 'God conscious.' We should spend time seeking the Lord and His anointing. There is a portion of Scripture in Isaiah chapter 61 that proves this to be correct and it says; "The Spirit of the Lord GOD is upon me; because the LORD hath anointed me to preach good tidings unto the meek; he hath sent me to bind up the brokenhearted, to proclaim liberty to the captives, and the opening of the prison to them that are bound; To proclaim the acceptable year of the LORD, and the day of vengeance of our God; to comfort all that mourn."

Did you know that there are six reasons to seek the anointing and that they are right here in this passage of Scripture? The whole reason to continue seeking for the anointing that the Lord has given us is right here, these first six things are the reason why you and I should see God everyday for fresh oil from his word.

1. That we could preach the good news of salvation
2. That we could bind up the brokenhearted
3. To proclaim liberty to the captives
4. To open prison doors to those who are bound
5. To proclaim the acceptable of the year of the Lord
      and the day of vengeance of our God
6. To comfort those who mourn.

Did you know that the acceptable year of the Lord is the year of Jubilee? It only happens once every 50 years. Most of us will only have one Jubilee in our lifetime. Jubilee means 'that every debt is canceled and everything that was taken was restored.' Think about the celebration you would have just knowing that you were going to get back the land that had been taken from you?

Are you wondering what the double portion is? The double portion that God wants to give us, even in affliction and hard times, is a double portion of joy. Many times, we think our double portion is given to us in the manner of material items and other "stuff." This is not true as it says in the book of Nehemiah *"that the joy of the Lord is my strength."* Therefore, if the enemy steals my joy he has my strength. Here is the bottom line the double portion blessing is having a double portion of joy. Remember, there is a difference between joy and happiness. Happiness depends on what is happening, while joy comes from within. You can have all kinds of heartache and trouble and still have joy in your soul through God's Holy Spirit.

I want to show you some things about the ligure stone. Remember, the Key Definition for *ligure* is "to engrave a seal." Let us look at three things that the engraving of a seal represents in the Bible. Also, how we have already been sealed and engraved by the Spirit of the Lord.

There is a story I want to go over with you in 1Kings chapter 21. There was a wicked king named Ahab, and his wife was the evil Jezebel. King Ahab had a beautiful palace and he looked out the window one morning and said, *"I would love to have the vineyard next to my palace so I can plant fresh herbs."* The king finds out that a man named Naboth owns the property. He goes to Naboth and says, *"Listen, I'm the King and your vineyard is right next to my palace and I want to buy it from you. I will give you a very good price for it or I will put you in another location."* Naboth told the king he could not do this, because the land had been in his family for generations. He wanted to leave the land it to his son. Naboth left the king and went home. Ahab did not like the response from Naboth. He went into the palace and threw himself on the bed, turned his face away, and he would not eat. The Bible says, *"he was sore displeased because he could not have what he wanted."* The word *"sore displeased"* found in verse 4 of this chapter means "to run out of humor." Jezebel came home and wanted to know what the king was doing lying on the bed, pouting with his long face to the wall. He answered by saying, "I can't have the vineyard next door, and I want it." Jezebel replies to the effect, "not to worry, I'll get it for you." So Jezebel writes a letter.

> 1Kings 21:7-9 *"And Jezebel his wife said unto him, Dost thou now govern the kingdom of Israel? Arise, and eat bread, and let thine heart be merry: I will give thee the vineyard of Naboth the Jezreelite. So she wrote letters in Ahab's name, and sealed them with his seal, and sent the letters unto the elders and to the nobles that were in his city, dwelling with Naboth. And she wrote in the letters, saying, proclaim a fast, and set Naboth on high among the people."*

The letter she wrote was a lie. Causing them to go out and kill this innocent man. Then they were able to steel his vineyard. This is what I want you to take note of, found in verse 8, what she did shows that they had absolute authority. The first point I want to make about the engraved seal is that it represents absolute authority. Due to the seal of nobles that was on the letter, it represented his absolute authority as King. This is why a *"seal"* in the Bible represents authority.

The second thing the *"seal"* represents can be found in the book of Nehemiah chapter 9. Remember that in Nehemiah chapter 8, 'the walls in the city were broken down, and gates were burned with fire.' Nehemiah was a Hebrew man taken into captivity in Babylon. The King let him go home to rebuild the walls and restore the gates around the city. After all of the repairs and restoration was completed, they had a large dedication. At the dedication, they happened to find the book of the Law that had been lost or buried in the rubble.

When they heard the word of God from the book of the Law, they repented; revival came along with a refilling. Then in Nehemiah chapter 9 it says, *"Now that God has restored us you have to get rid of your pagan wives, you have to honor the Sabbath and keep it holy, and I want to make a covenant so that you'll do these things."* Here is what happens at the end of all this. Look what happens at the end of the chapter 9 verse 38, *"And because of all this we make a sure covenant, and write it; and our princes, Levites, and priests, seal unto it."*

This is the second point about being engraved with a seal, not only do you have authority; it also means that you have a covenant. Here is the important point out of Nehemiah, 'there is a covenant that has been written down and sealed with authority.'

Finally, we have to know where to find our seal and where we can find our covenant. It can be found in Song of Solomon chapter 8 verse 6. Let us look at the beginning of this verse. The bride says this to the groom, her beloved; *"set me as a seal upon your heart and as a seal upon thine arm."* We have been sealed in our hearts. The seal of the authority and the seal of the covenant are in our hearts.

Three things the engraving seal represents to us who are in Christ Jesus. Number one Authority; number two, Covenant Assurance in our hearts; and number three, Righteousness.

What does a seal do? Have you ever tried to get a seal off a medicine bottle? Do you know how hard it is to get that cap off? I know that they are supposed be childproof proof, but I am an adult and sometimes I have to get the Rubbermaid bottle opener to get the top off. The longer the seal has been on the bottle the tighter the protection. We are already sealed and I am so glad. Let me show you your seal in the New Testament. You have been sealed upon your heart. What is that seal that has been engraved upon us?

Romans 4:11 *"And he received the sign of circumcision, a seal of the righteousness of the faith which he had yet being uncircumcised: that he might be the father of all them that believe, though they be not circumcised; that righteousness might be imputed unto them also"*

Circumcision was to cut the blood and it meant that you had a right relationship with God. In this verse, look at this, 'that even before Abraham was circumcised he had a seal of righteousness.' Do you understand that we do not have to be circumcised in our flesh anymore? We have been circumcised, in our heart by God's Spirit. This gives us the seal of righteousness, if we could only get a hold of this. Because we do not see it and because sometimes we do not act righteous, this hinders us.

2 Corinthians 1:21-22 *"Now He which established us with you in Christ, and hath anointed us, is God; and Who hath also sealed us, and given the earnest of the Spirit in our hearts."*

Not only are we sealed, but also we have been given an anointing. There are a couple of definitions for anointing in the Greek *"chiro,"* which means "to thoroughly furnish." Here is an example: when I go to speak at other locations; they furnish me with a podium for my Bible and a stand for the microphone. Nevertheless, unless I teach the Bible or speak, the equipment does not do me any good.

The second word for anointing in the bible is not *"chrio"* to supply what I need, but it is the word *"charisma"* which means, "the gifting to use, which is provided." How grateful I am that not only has the Lord anointed us, but He has also given us the gifting to use the powerful anointing that abides in each of us. In Romans 4:11 we are *"sealed in righteousness,"* and in 2 Corinthians 1:21-22 the *"Holy Spirit Himself seals us."*

Have you ever seen a horse or a steer when they are being branded? Branding is to mark an animal for ownership. They are identified by the brand, which is registered to the owner. Once a brand has been burned into the animals hide, it is there forever. They are marked for life. Bottom line, we are sealed, just like that. By the Spirit of God, we have been sealed and we belong to the kingdom of God.

Ephesians 1:12-13 *"That we should be to the praise of his glory, who first trusted in Christ. In whom ye also trusted, after that ye heard the word of truth, the gospel of your salvation: in whom also after that ye believed, ye were sealed with that Holy Spirit of promise"*

I want to show here that not only are we sealed to be righteous by the

Holy Spirit, but that we actually have a promise. We are sealed with a promise from God. We are actually sealed with a promise of our inheritance. When someone dies without a will, it can get ugly and sometimes ungodly. Everyone begins to fight over the inheritance. Family members begin to act like strangers and demand their rights. No matter what the outcome they know how important an inheritance can be. We need to be so grateful that Jesus left us His will and testament, so we can receive our inheritance. We are allowed to enter in and receive all that God prepared for us because we are marked and sealed by Him.

Ephesians 4:30 will show you that we are sealed to an event. *"And grieve not the Holy Spirit of God, whereby ye are sealed unto the day of redemption."* The scripture is saying to us that the Holy Spirit has sealed us and that we have been redeemed. Jesus paid it all and God wants to freely give us all things.

I am so glad that I can be fruitful even in affliction and that the enemy has been exposed; the thief has been caught and God will repay and redeem.

I found out that since I was a child of God. I have a double portion of joy and a double portion of blessing. Just holding on to this gives the enemy no hold in your life. You and I have been purchased with a price by the precious blood of Jesus. Everything the enemy has tried to steal from our lives must be restored to us because Jesus came to give us an abundant life, a double portion, and a double blessing of joy.

When we are sealed, we have Authority, Righteousness, and Promises from God as we await the day of Redemption.

2 Timothy 2:19-21 *"Nevertheless the foundation of God standeth sure, having this seal, The Lord knoweth them that are his. And, let everyone that nameth the name of Christ depart from iniquity. But in a great house there are not only vessels of gold and of silver, but also of wood and of earth; and some to honour, and some to dishonour. If a man therefore purge himself from these, he shall be a vessel unto honour, sanctified, and meet for the master's use, and prepared unto every good work."*

The choice is yours. You have been sealed unto Christ, for the day of redemption. Therefore, we need to choose to become a vessel of honor. This scripture tells us 'there are vessels of gold and silver, wood and earth, all the vessels are important and useful.' All of these vessels have a use, and some had a higher purpose. If you were going to give me a breadbasket that was made out of wicker or you bought me a real gold bowl with an assortment of bread, which do you think I would prefer to use?

I would kick the wicker basket to the curb and pick up the gold bowl. I would not even look at the wicker basket, because I know how valuable gold is. The Bible teaches us that because we are sealed to Christ that we should get rid of the things in our lives that contaminate us. That we can go before Him and say, 'Lord, I want to be a pure vessel. I want to be a vessel of honor, fit for the Master's use. I always want You to be honored in my life.'

## Key Points

Hold onto this that the enemy will not have any right to your life if you would only begin to say, "Wait a minute! I am sealed and I have been redeemed! I have been purchased with a price by the precious Blood of Jesus. For that reason, Satan, you must restore everything you have stolen out of my life! In Jesus' Name, Amen"

Always remember, Jesus came to give you abundant life, a double portion of blessing. Jesus paid it all and God wants to freely give you all things. As a son or daughter of God, you are entitled to a double portion of joy, and a double portion of blessing!

## Closing Prayer

*Father, I thank You for the blessing. Thank You that even in our infirmities or weakness, we have been sealed with your precious Spirit. God, even as Ephraim was doubly fruitful in affliction, so even in the hard times in my life You will give me double joy if I just seek You. Help me to find the thief out so that he gets away with nothing, because I have been sealed with the Holy Spirit of God. I am sealed with the promise. I am sealed for the Day of Redemption. I am sealed unto Christ. Thank You for You are my King and You set Your seal upon my heart by Your Spirit. I just ask that You would be glorified and honored in my life and that no matter what afflic-tion I have to go through, I would not be resentful or angry, bitter, or un-forgiving. In Jesus Name, Amen!*

# CHAPTER 9

# *– The Eighth Stone –*
# *The Agate of Manasseh*

*Father, once again, we just want to thank You for the Word of God. Thank You and we ask You to bless us, Father just pray that the Holy Spirit will be our teacher and that He would enlighten us and illuminate us. Father, we realize that we are a living priesthood and the royal holy nation. We pray that we would be polished and that people would see the light of the Gospel in each of our live In Jesus Name, Amen.*

We have reached the third row of stones in the breastplate of the high priest and in this chapter we will be covering the second stone of the third row. This second stone, which is agate, comes from the tribe of *Manasseh.*

We have already covered the first stone in the third row of the breastplate from our previous chapter and that stone was the ligure stone from the tribe of *Ephraim.* As you may recall, it means that we have been sealed with the Holy Spirit for a double portion. This chapter is about *Manasseh* and his stone and story. Remember, *Ephraim* and *Manasseh* were not one of the original twelve sons. They are grandsons of Jacob and sons of Joseph. Please make a mental note that the main point of this book is to show you what Peter is saying; 'that we are living stones, a royal priesthood.' through the stones placed in the breastplate.

The Key Definition for *Manasseh* is "helping me to forget the past." God knows that we can all use a *Manasseh* in our lives. It is interesting that Manasseh is the firstborn, but Ephraim, the second born, is the first stone represented on the breastplate. Therefore, *Manasseh* means "God helped me to forget my past" and *Ephraim* means, "double fruitful in affliction." When we begin to go back in our minds to things that are painful or hurtful from our past, God is gracious enough to remind us of the following, 'I want you to forget your past injuries because I can't bless you in the mist of your pain.'

Almost everyone knows the story of Joseph and how he was a favored son. We covered this in previous chapters as well. Let us refresh a bit. Joseph was sold into slavery and sold into bondage where he was incarcerated for about thirteen years. His incarceration ended when he was thirty years old. Pharaoh wanted to reward Joseph for all of his great work so he gave him a wife. She was an Egyptian woman, and together they had two children.

> Genesis 41:51 *"And Joseph called the name of the firstborn Manasseh: For God, said he, hath made me forget all my toil, and my entire father's house."*

The second stone in the third row of the breastplate is the agate stone, we see it mentioned in Exodus chapter 28 verse19, "And the third row a ligure, an agate, and an amethyst."

The Key definition for *agate* is "streams of flames." The agate is a blend of many colors and is not mentioned too many times in the Bible. One of the scriptures I found where it describes what the agate stone is in Isaiah 54. Isaiah shows us that if we could blend in with God we would look just like the agate.

> Isaiah 54:11-13 *"O thou afflicted, tossed with tempest, and not comforted, behold, I will lay thy stones with fair colors, and lay thy foundations with sapphires. And I will make thy windows of agates, and thy gates of carbuncles, and all thy borders of pleasant stones. And all thy children shall be taught of the LORD; and great shall be the peace of thy children."*

I have taken the time to study this topic and, every time I see a stone in Scripture, I take time out to learn about the color and its meaning. Do you remember that the word sapphire means "to polish?" Therefore, in verse 11 God is saying 'that even the foundations of our lives He wants to polish and make beautiful.' Now in verse 12, it says an *agate* is a "window." The word *window* means "sunlight" or "to let in sunlight." The agate stone is a window therefore we need to allow the light into every area of our lives. Not only do we have streams, but also we have flames of His Spirit. I looked up every Scripture I could find on windows and this familiar Scripture spoke volumes to me.

> Malachi 3:10 *"Bring ye all the tithes into the storehouse, that there may be meat in mine house, and prove me now herewith, saith the LORD of hosts, if I will not open you the windows of heaven, and pour you out a blessing, that there shall not be room enough to receive it."*

The Lord wants to open the windows of heaven and pour out a Blessing on us; He wants His house to be a house of provisions for the nations. Personally I feel that the more we blend together and the more we remove the prejudices, racism, age discrimination, sexual discrimination, and financial discrimination, the more we become one with Jesus. The clearer the window is the more light we get and the more flames of fire we are going to have in our lives.

I can't wait to show you this incredible blessing bestowed on Manasseh from Moses in Deuteronomy chapter 33. I want to show you that *Manasseh* actually means to "push people together," another meaning is "forgetting the pain of our past" and the word *agate* means "streams of flames."

> Isaiah 54:12 *"And I will make thy windows of agates, and thy gates of carbuncles, and all thy borders of pleasant stones."*

This is one of the very few verses in the Bible a about the agate stone, do you see that is state's 'God is going to make our windows of agate.' God wants to open up the windows of heaven for us so that His light can shine through our lives. In Hebrew, the word is *"shemesh"* which means to let the sun come in, the rising of the sun and the setting of the sun.

> Deuteronomy 33:16-17 *"And for the precious things of the earth and fullness thereof, and for the good will of him that dwelt in the bush: let the blessing come upon the head of Joseph, and upon the top of the head of him that was separated from his brethren. His glory is like the firstling of his bullock, and his horns are like the horns of unicorns: with them he shall push the people together to the ends of the earth: and they are the ten*

*thousands of Ephraim, and they are the thousands of Manasseh."*

In this particular blessing from Moses, he actually speaks of Joseph and his sons bringing people together from all the ends of the earth, and God compares this to the push of a unicorn. A unicorn is a mythological creature, usually described as a horse with a horn in the center of his head and in some circumstances; a ring appears around the head of the unicorn. I believe that unicorns are fictitious. The word unicorn is the original word for oxen, or a strong bull. Therefore, when I look at the blessing that Moses gave these two grandsons, the only thing I could find was that their whole purpose was to push people together. Understand that because we are all blended, only the Spirit of the Lord can put us together or push us together.

God pushes us together because the young have something for the old and the old have something for the young. All of us are from different cultures, we can have different customs, and we should glean so much from one another. I grew up in a White home and had White neighbors and I knew nothing about African-Americans. I remember one time I went to the Virgin Islands to speak and all of the women there were African-American. A home opened up to us with many bedrooms and our accommodations were lovely. As they prepared my bedding and toiletries, I was only given one towel. I said, "I needed two towels please." I remember one of my friends asking why I needed two towels and I said, "because I wash my hair every day." She said "you do what?" I repeated that I wash my hair every day and said to her, "don't you wash your hair every day?" She said, "if she washed her hair every day she would be completely bald; because the oil in her hair is different from mine and washing it every day would damage her hair." Once she explained this, we laughed together. That night when they came out, they had stockings on their heads. This was something I had never seen, but I learned to adjust for the unity of the Spirit in a bond of peace. Instead of being threatened, by differences, we need to embrace them. God is a Spirit and in the Spirit, we all look exactly like Him.

One of the problems is that we judge one another based on appearance. We all should memorize the following Scripture.

2 Corinthians 5:17 *"if any man be in Christ he is a new creation. The old things are passed away, and all things become new."*

Do you remember the verse in front of it? Verse 16 goes like this, *"we look at no man in the flesh any longer."* This scripture ministers to me. Another scripture tells us that He makes all things new. Yet, we still look at each other in the flesh. No matter who we are, we have to forget our past and look at each other through the eyes of the Spirit.

We have to get pushed together this is why every one of us needs a Manasseh in our life. I did a retreat recently and I felt the Lord speak to me that we needed to break down the barriers of racism. There were 150 women at the conference. The Spirit of the Lord was bold upon me and I just told them "I needed them to forgive me and my race, because of things done to their race, and everyone ended up crying." I got to thinking about how we talk about the Black race and the White race, the Hispanic race, and the Asian race. There is only one race and it is the human. Who made all of these divisions? Man not God. God created humanity which is called the human race. I do not know what happened to divide us; the one thing I do know is that God wants us together and the enemy wants us apart. Why are we letting the enemy separate us? God determined all the men would live on the earth "by one blood." Do you see according to Acts the blood makes all humanity one.

Acts 17:26 *"And hath made of one blood all nations of men for to dwell on all the face of the earth, and hath determined the times before appointed, and the bounds of their habitation;"*

According to Numbers, chapter 24 unicorns have tremendous strength. Manasseh used the strength of the unicorn or oxen to push people together.

Numbers 24:8 *"God brought him forth out of Egypt; he hath as it were the strength of a unicorn: he shall eat up the nations his enemies, and shall break their bones, and pierce them through with his arrows."*

God showed me something fascinating in Psalm 92:10, *"But my horn shalt thou exalt like the horn of an unicorn: I shall be anointed with fresh oil."* I have known this scripture, and I have talked about this verse but I never really noticed this until I started writing this book. What David is saying in this verse is the horn of the ox or unicorn was used for the anointing oil. Whether a person has a different background, or a different race, or has a different education, none of this matters to God. You do not have to push me to accept others; I am willing to do so because I want the anointing. Nothing will quench the anointing quicker than having a poor attitude or a wrong heart.

Have you ever noticed in 1 Samuel chapter 10 verse 1, that when the prophet Samuel anointed King Saul he used a man made container called "a flask or a vial?" This king was the people's choice; however, Gods choice would be to anoint King David. In 1 Samuel chapter 16 verse 1 it speaks about the anointing of King David, it's says 'to fill the horn with oil.' Do you notice the difference in how the kings were anointed? The people's choice used a man made container. Whereas, Gods choice required the death of animal, and the sacrifice of blood in order for the anointing oil to flow from the horn of a unicorn.

There are three things; I want to mention to give you a better understanding of the tribe of Manasseh, which means 'causing to forget the past.'

Isaiah 43:18-19 *"Remember ye not the former things, neither consider the things of old. Behold, I will do a new thing; now it shall spring forth; shall ye not know it? I will even make a way in the wilderness, and rivers in the desert."*

What is God telling us in verse 18? God is telling us to forget the old things and to forget the past. Do you know how many people live in the past? Some people are so caught up; in their past lives, they forget to enjoy the present and certainly cannot focus on future. We need to make a decision to step out of the past and to step into today. I like how my husband puts it, "our past is like the rear view mirror in our car, and our future is like the windshield." We may need to glace back every now and then to learn from the past; however, our focus should remain on the present and future. Please understand this, if you live in the past, you ruin your present, and it takes all the joy and hope out of your future. We all have a past; thank God for the Blood of Jesus. I took the liberty of looking up the word remember in verse 18 and it means 'to deliberately recall something to your mind.' God clearly states in this scripture not to consider things from our past.

Listen, if you and I are stuck in the past we bind God up. When these things come to mind, the Bible says to take every thought captive. It is decision time! When these thoughts come to mind, you have to make a decision to renew your mind taking captive every thought and bring it into the obedience of Christ. Therefore, whenever I have a painful thought from my past, I have learned to give it over to God.

Let me share a testimony of how God recently healed a painful memory for me. My granddaughter has a horse and she asked me, "Mom-mom, would you like to ride my horse?" I said, "No, Kristina, I don't want to ride your horse Hayden because I've had some bad experiences." My granddaughter asked me "what happened to you that you don't want to ride my horse?" I told her "when I was about eight years old, my next-door neighbor Carol had won a horse in a contest. The whole neighborhood was excited because Carol had won a horse. Every morning I would go over to Carol's house and help her and her father renovate the garage into a stable. We had to get hay, a trough, and some feedbags. The day came for the horse to be delivered, and Carol's Dad allowed all of the neighborhood kids to take a ride. I anxiously awaited my turn and when the time came for me to ride; her dad said, 'You can't ride this horse! You're too fat and you'll break his back.' The crushing part of the story for me was that he said this in front of all of the other children in the neighborhood. They all began to laugh at me, and I got this huge lump in my throat and I ran home sobbing. I never did ride her horse." Kristina then said to me, "Mom-mom, that is a very sad story and I promise if you were to ride my horse you would not hurt it." I told her how much I appreciated her understanding and said, "I love you and know now as an adult that he was kidding, but it surely hurt me that day." When I started studying this stone of Manasseh and learning how to overcome the past I decide to go to the horse farm with Kristina again and take her up on her offer. I was able to overcome my fears of the past and take a ride on Hayden. Neither he nor I suffered any injury that day and my granddaughter was proud of me. I was able to show her that standing in God's word for my future was more important than looking in the rear view mirror at the past.

Some of you might be too young to remember how we used to use blotters in school instead erasers. With a blotter, you would absorb up the ink from an old-fashioned ink pen whenever a mistake was made. In the Scripture below, there is a cool statement about God blotting out your sin.

Isaiah 43:25 *"I, even I, am he that blotted out thy transgressions for mine own sake, and will not remember thy sins."*

Now here is the point, once you use a blotter the words are no longer legible there is no way to decipher what was once written because the mistake has been eradicated. Can you get it into your spirit that once God blots out your sins, He says they are gone? He no longer remembers them and neither should we.

The final item I want to reveal to you is something that I had to live out. We have to forget the shame of our youth.

Isaiah 54:4 *"Fear not; for thou shalt not be ashamed: neither be thou confounded; for thou shalt not be put to shame: for thou shalt forget the shame of thy youth, and shalt not remember the reproach of thy widowhood anymore."*

I get emotional even when I think of how awesome this scripture has been in my life. I was sexually abuse in my childhood. From that experience, a spirit of shame had entered into me. I always felt that something was wrong with me and I never knew why. When I became a married woman, my mother had shared some things about this abuse. After that conversation with her, the Lord opened up the Scripture in Isaiah 54. Once I let this Scripture enter into my spirit I prayed to the Lord asking Him to deliver me from a spirit of shame. What a glorious deliverance I had! If you feel like you have a spirit of shame then take it to the Lord. Take time to pray Isaiah 54 in your life so that you are not going to bear the shame of your youth anymore.

Like Manasseh, we need to forget our past and know that God has a bright future for us and a wonderful present, that we can learn to enjoy. We need to stop calling to mind our past sins that we have been forgiven of, because as you know, we cannot go back and change anything. How many of us have said, "If I can only go back and change this!" We cannot! You and I are just wasting energy and time, because there is not a thing in the world that we can do that could change one thing that has already been done. If you do what God says in Philippians He will help us forget our past.

Philippians 3:13 *"This one thing I do, forgetting what's behind, I press on to the high calling of God, which is Christ Jesus."*

We choose to do this not the Holy Spirit, not God, not Jesus; this one thing I do. I choose to forget the past, pressing on to the mark of the high calling in Christ Jesus. I thought since our lesson is about Manasseh and causing us to forget our past, it might be nice to go through some people and just mention some things that they had to forget from their past.

For example, Moses had to forget his past Moses had to forget that he was a killer when he wrote the Ten Commandments, "thou shalt not kill." Have you ever really thought about what it must have felt like when God came to Moses and said, "Thou shall not kill?" This is one thing that we know for sure that Moses did he killed an Egyptian. Moses buried his body in the sand and he tried to bury his sin along with it.

The next person we will look at is Jacob. Before he wrestled with God, he was a liar, a cheater, and a deceiver. He lied to his dying father, he deceived his brother while steeling his birthright. Jacobs's character was in need of great improvement and yet God said, "I am the God of Abraham, Isaac and Jacob." He had to forget what he did to his brother Esau, and to his dying father. Even Jacob's mother told him to run away until his brother Esau's anger was abated. He ran for some twenty years before God told him to go home. He did not want to go meet his brother Esau, but Esau's heart was already softened. He returned home and was reconciled with his brother and together they released the past.

The next one I want to bring to your attention is Joseph. He is one of my favorite Old Testament heroes and his life so relates to the life of Jesus. The first verse about Joseph in Genesis 37 says that his brothers hated him and never spoke a kind word to him. He had to forget his childhood. Remember, they hated him and they never ever spoke a kind word to him. He named his two sons fruitful in affliction and God has caused me to forget the pain of my past. He is a good example of what we need to do.

Let me show you what happens to Gideon. Gideon was terrified by fear. In Judges chapter 6, you see him hiding in a winepress. He was afraid of the Midianites. There are people who are afraid of getting on elevators, getting on a train, flying in a plane, or even going out of their homes. We all have fears and Gideon had to forget this fear.

There is a woman in the Old Testement that also had a sorted past that needed to be released. Rahab was a woman of the night, a prostitute. Rahab had to forget her impurity, fornication, adultery, and sin. Jesus said, "the prostitutes and the whoremongers come into the kingdom of God faster than the righteous." This is true even today. There have been many who have chosen a life of drugs, alcohol, and sex; yet, when they turn their life to Christ they are released from the shame of their past.

King David for example committed adultery with Bathsheba and then murdered her husband Uriah, a mighty man who served King David. Because of these sins the child conceived between Bathsheba and King David was sentenced to die. King David fell to the ground, fasted, and prayed for seven days, "God please don't kill this innocent baby." After the seven day fast Kind David is made aware of the child's passing. King David rose up to go and clean himself off; once cleaned he went into the temple to worship. I do not know about you, but if my baby died, especially if I felt responsible for it, I do not know if I could go and worship. I thought oh my Lord, we have to learn to forget the past and focus our worship on God.

Then I thought about Peter, he denied the Lord and began to call down curses. Any one of us is capable of saying a curse word. He had to forget his denial of the Lord and his bad language.

There is a story that was brought to my remembrance of a time that I cursed at my mother. My punishment was to have my mouth washed out with soap; to this day I cannot use Ivory soap even though it is 99.9% pure.

Remember John Mark, he was the nephew of Barnabas. Let me tell you what he did so you know what he had to forget. John Mark went on a mission's trip with Barnabas and Saul. In the middle of the mission, John Mark felt that it was too much for him and he needed a bath or a hot shower. He needed a Holiday Inn. He decided he could not take it anymore, eating locusts and bugs, and he needed to go home. John Mark left the mission field.

Years later in Acts 15, Barnabas told Paul he decided to go back and visit churches that they had established. Barnabas wanted to take John Mark with them and Paul said no. These two men of God had a big argument and they separated. John Mark was responsible for the separation between Paul and Barnabas. John Mark was guilty of bringing division to the body of Christ. Once he let go of his past God was able to utilize him in pinning the New Testament book that we know as the Gospel Mark. I rejoice in what the Lord has done in John Mark's life and how he was able to overcome a bad decision from his past.

Mary Magdalene had seven demonic spirits cast out of her. I do not know what were are and I am not going to make any conjecture. Jesus cast out these unclean spirits. Let me show you the magnitude of her deliverance, because there was not one, not two, not three, not four, not five, not six, but seven demonic spirits tormenting her. How would you like to live with that as your reputation? Yet, this Mary is the one that Jesus first appeared to when he rose from the dead.

Do any of these stories reflect something in your past? Can you comprehend that God uses murderers, prostitutes, adulterers, liars, cheaters, thieves, and people that were once under Satan's bondage. I pray that as you have read this, hope has risen in your heart. If we can do one thing, let it be to forget what is in our past and press on to the mark of the high calling.

## Key Points

- If you live in the past, you will ruin your present and delay your future
- Forget the sins of your past that you have renounced and confessed
- Forget the shame of your youth

## Closing Prayer

*Father, thank You for the Word of God. Lord, I thank You that the Bible says "This one thing I do, forgetting what is behind, I press on to the mark of the high calling" and so, Lord, thank You for the Holy Spirit. Lord, today, like Manasseh, I choose to forget the past and press on. I pray that*

*You would open the windows of heaven and pour out a blessing so that the light of your Son would come and the fire and flames of your Holy Spirit would be alive within me. Lord, as I pray I am reminded of how good and pleasant it is when brethren are drawn together in unity, which it is like the precious oil running down Aaron's beard all the way to the hem of his garment. Lord, also I am reminded that where there is unity, I will find your blessing. Help me to live in unity and with a right spirit towards all men. In Jesus Name, Amen.*

# CHAPTER 10

## – The Nineth Stone –
## The Amethyst of Benjamin

*Father, thank You for the freedom to study Your Word and we thank You that Your Word will endure through all generations. As we look at the third stone in the third row, I pray that you would enlighten us as we study about the amethyst from the tribe of Benjamin. Cause us to take the information we are learning to heart and realize that we are living stones, a royal priesthood that should show forth the praises of Him that has called us out of darkness and into Your marvelous light. We thank You, for illuminating us with your truth. In Jesus name, Amen.*

The third row of stones is the one that inspired this entire book to be written, it all began when I was reading Ezekiel Chapter 28. The third row of stones is the row the enemy does not have. This was the Word of the Lord about *Lucifer,* and the sin of his rebellion. Whose name means, "the bright star of the morning." In Ezekiel, God has some impressive things to reveal to us in this passage of Scripture. The order of the stones listed in Ezekiel chapter 28 verses 13-15, do not line up exactly as they are recorded in the book of Exodus on the breastplate of the highest priest.

Ezekiel 28:13-15 *"Thou hast been in Eden the garden of God; every precious stone was thy covering, the Sardius, topaz, and the diamond, the beryl, the onyx, and the jasper, the sapphire, the emerald, and the carbuncle, and gold: the workmanship of thy labrets and of thy pipes was prepared in thee in the day that thou wast created. Thou art the anointed cherub*

*that covered; and I have set thee so: thou wast upon the holy mountain of*
*God; thou hast walked up and down in the midst of the stones of fire.*
*Thou wast perfect in thy ways from the day that thou wast created, till*
*iniquity was found in thee."*

The first stone in the third row from left to right would have been a ligure stone from the tribe of Ephraim. The second stone would have been the agate of Manasseh. In this chapter, we are studying the amethyst of the tribe of *Benjamin.* What is so interesting about this is that the definition of *Manasseh* means, "to cause me to forget all of the pain of my past." The enemy does not have the capability to forget his past; there is no redemption for him. He will forever be reminded of what he lost because of his rebellion. He does not have the stone of Manasseh, which would cause him to forget the pain of his past. He certainly does not have the stone of *Ephraim,* which means, "double fruit in your affliction." In addition, he definitely does not have the stone of *Benjamin.*

> Genesis 35:16-20 *"Then they journeyed from Bethel. Moreover, when*
> *there was but a little distance to go to Ephrath, Rachel labored in child-*
> *birth, and she had hard labor. Now it came to pass, when she was in hard*
> *labor, that the midwife said to her, "Do not fear; you will have this son*
> *also." Therefore, it was, as her soul was departing (for she died), that she*
> *called his name Ben-Oni; but his father called him Benjamin. Therefore,*
> *Rachel died and was buried on the way to Ephrath (that is, Bethlehem).*
> *And Jacob set a pillar on her grave, which is the pillar of Rachel's grave to*
> *this day."*

Where did Benjamin receive his name and why is this so important to us? Because, Jacob only had two sons by his lovely wife Rachel. The first-born was *Joseph,* which means, "God will add to me another son." Then Rachel gets pregnant with this child, which Jacob had to rename Benjamin. As she lay dying, she names her son Ben-Oni. The name *Ben-Oni* means, "son of all my sorrow." That might have been the very last thing that she ever spoke before her passing. Jacob said no, we would change his name to *Benjamin,* which means, "the son of my right hand." Did you know that Jesus is at the right hand of the Father, so Satan cannot hold that position? He is not God's right hand man. Jesus became a man of sorrows much like Ben-Oni was prior to his name change. And Isaiah tells us, *"He was a man of sorrows and acquainted with grief: and we hid as it were our faces from him;*

*he was despised, and we esteemed him not."* After Jesus bore our sorrows, he ascended and is now seated at the right-hand of God.

The ninth stone the amethyst of the tribe of Benjamin is a beautiful, dark purple stone. The darker the purple is, the better the stone. The Key Definition for *amethyst* is "to dream." Many men and women of God were given dreams throughout the Bible.

The first one who comes to mind is Jacob. When Jacob fled the scene from his father and ran from his brother, in Genesis chapter 28 verse 11 Jacob decides to lie down to take a nap. Do you remember the dream? It is called Jacob's ladder! I never really did know about the dream until I heard people talking about. In this dream heaven opened up and he saw the angels ascending and descending. During this dream, he encounter God. He named the place where he had the dream *"Bethel."* It is very interesting because this is the very place where Rachel, Jacobs's wife, died.

I thought about his son Joseph, how his whole problem started when he had a dream from God. Then I thought about Pharaoh and how he had a dream and only Joseph could interpret the dream. In the New Testament, Joseph had an angel appear to him twice in a dream, telling him to take Jesus to Egypt. While they were in Egypt, Joseph had another dream telling him that it would be safe for them to take Jesus back home. Another person in the New Testament that had dreams was Paul the apostle who had dreams and visions. I trust you know that dreams and visions have always been in the plan of God. It is not uncommon for people to have a dreams or visions. I want you to understand that whenever it comes from the realm of the supernatural or you are sleeping, you become open to other influences. You have to use wisdom in discerning the meaning of a dream. Not every dream you have is from God, as we have all had strange and weird dreams. For this reason, I find myself unmoved by dreams unless I really, truly, know that it is from God. Being saved for over many years, I have had only two dreams that I know were something God wanted for me.

I want to show you two verses describing what the color purple stands for in the Scriptures since the amethyst is purple. There was a young man by the name of *Gideon.* He was afraid of the Midianites and an angel appeared to him calling him the "mighty man of valor." God tells Gideon to go save Israel with his strength. Gideon has some fears and concerns and says, "God, if this is really what you want me to do I will obey." Gideon, with 300 men acquires a great victory slaying the Midianites. However, two of their kings escaped, Gideon heads out to find these escaped kings to slay them. He accomplishes this mission and as a reward, the people want to elevate him. As we see in Judges chapter 8.

> Judges 8:22-23 *"Then the men of Israel said unto Gideon, Rule thou over us, both thou, and thy son, and thy son's son also: for thou hast delivered us from the hand of Midian. And Gideon said unto them, I will not rule over you, neither shall my son rule over you: the LORD shall rule over you."*

I really wish that the chapter had stopped, right there because Gideon had a wonderful beginning and a horrible ending. What he does next is just an awful thing. Gideon continues to say unto them;

> Judges 8:24-26 *"I would desire a request of you, that ye would give me every man the earrings of his prey. (For they had golden earrings because they were Ishmaelites.) In addition, they answered, we will willingly give them. Moreover, they spread a garment, and did cast therein every man the earrings of his prey. And the weight of the golden earrings that he requested was a thousand and seven hundred shekels of gold; beside ornaments, and collars, and purple raiment that was on the kings of Midian, and beside the chains that were about their camels' necks."*

Did you see in verse 26, it actually says that kings of royalty wore purple. It was not a common color. Only if you were wealthy, or if you were of prominence would you be able to wear this particular color. Following along in the story of Gideon, I want to show you what happens next.

> Judges 8:27-28 *"And Gideon made an ephod thereof, and put it in his city, even in Ophrah: and all Israel went thither a whoring after it: which thing became a snare unto Gideon, and to his house. Thus was Midian subdued before the children of Israel, so that they lifted up their heads no more. And the country was in quietness forty years in the days of Gideon."*

How awful it was for Gideon to make an ephod, a memorial statue, to himself. Absalom and Nebuchadnezzar did the same thing. This action always brought sin to Israel. What I realized through reading their stories is that you can have a fabulous beginning and a dreadful end. I decided that even though my beginning was rough, I plan to have a great ending. Their example really puts the fear of God in me, how about you.

Let us look in the New Testament at Luke chapter 16 verse 19. You will be very familiar with this story. In this parable, there is a very wealthy man and a beggar; look at what happens to these two men and the apparel of the wealthy man.

Luke 16:19-21 *"There was a certain rich man, which was clothed in purple and fine linen, and fared sumptuously every day: And there was a certain beggar named Lazarus, which was laid at his gate, full of sores, And desiring to be fed with the crumbs which fell from the rich man's table."*

Did you notice that the rich man was clothed in purple and fine linen? In those days purple was not a common color, one had to be extremely wealthy or be of royalty, in order to wear it.

I have shown you are two Scripture references one from the Old Testament and one from the New Testament proving that purple is the color of royalty. It is symbolic of authority, prominence, and great wealth. As you may recall, the Key Definition for *Benjamin* is "son of my right hand." Many of us know that Jesus is seated at the Father's right hand. Can you picture what Jesus is wearing while seated at the right hand God; his robe in fine linen made of purple thread.

I want to show you a couple of things in the Old Testament that happened from that position and then we are going to look at the New Testament.

Exodus 15:1-6 *"Then sang Moses and the children of Israel this song unto the LORD, and spake, saying, I will sing unto the LORD, for he hath triumphed gloriously: the horse and his rider hath he thrown into the sea. The LORD is my strength and song, and he is become my salvation: he is my God, and I will prepare him an habitation; my father's God, and I will exalt him. The LORD is a man of war: the LORD is his name. Pharaoh's chariots and his host hath he cast into the sea: his chosen captains also are drowned in the Red sea. The depths have covered them: they sank into the bottom as a stone. Thy right hand, O LORD, is become glorious in power: thy right hand, O LORD, hath dashed in pieces the enemy."*

In this story, the children of God had just come out of Egypt. They crossed the Red Sea and they were preparing to celebrate. Did you notice that the words of this Scripture have become a song that we used to sing in worship gatherings? In my Bible, wherever I would come across a song we used to sing, I would put two little music notes next to it to remind myself the song came from that Scripture. One day my husband borrowed my Bible and wanted to know what all of these little music notes were doing next to the Scriptures. He hysterically laughed because my music notes look like little tadpoles. I love being able to sing the Word of God.

At the end of the section in Scripture, we notice that the right hand is a position of power and victory. In verse 7, it speaks of them being overthrown and consumed.

In Psalm chapter 17, we will see another event that happens at the right hand. I want to say that in the Bible the left hand was considered to be unclean. The only way I can explain this to you is that in the biblical days and even in some third world countries today, they do not have the facilities that we have in America. When I was in India, I found that they did not have any public restrooms. We had been on a bus for about five hours when a woman asked if we could stop at a rest area. The bus driver just chuckled. We found out that they do not have rest stops, we had to get out of the bus and use the open street for your bodily functions. Since these third world countries do not have any toilet tissue, they must use their left hand. I learned early on that you never put your left hand on the table. You can have fifteen people at the table and if you put your left hand on the table, the table has been defiled. All through the Bible, it speaks of the right hand because since early times the left hand was considered unsanitary.

Psalm 17:6-7 *"I have called upon thee, for thou wilt hear me, O God: incline thine ear unto me, and hear my speech. Shew thy marvelous loving kindness, O thou that saves by thy right hand them which put their trust in thee from those that rise up against them."*

Therefore, we see here in the Scripture that anyone who puts their trust in the right hand of God finds salvation. The right hand is a place of salvation. By Jesus sitting at the right hand of God, it is the place where salvation is given.

Psalm 48:10 *"According to thy name, O God, so is thy praise unto the ends of the earth: thy right hand is full of righteousness."*

Lucifer does not have a righteous position because he does not offer salvation or sit at anyone's right hand. As seen in the above verse the right hand is full of righteousness and victory. Righteousness simply put means 'that we are in right standing with God.'

Many people confuse the word righteousness with sanctification. The Lord is my sanctification. Some people believe that sanctification is something that happens on the outside. In reality, sanctification is something that happens on the inside, affecting your outside. Sanctification is the work of the Holy Spirit on the inside of you that produces holiness; it is an internal work. Righteousness is not found within ourselves. One instance that comes to mind is where you see the Pharisee and the Publican praying in the Bible. The Pharisee was self-righteous and he said, "I give a tenth of all I have, I read the Torah and I am faithful to go to synagogue." The Publican put his head down and beat his chest in humility. Jesus said, "Which one of these received mercy of God?" It was not the self-righteous Pharisee but the Publican sinner. I think the real lost son in the prodigal story is the elder brother far more than the younger brother. The younger brother knew he was going to be lost so he went out, repented, and came back. The older brother was lost because he was so self-righteous that the Scripture says he would not even go into his father's house. He was so angry that he stayed on the outside of the celebration. Anger keeps us out of the presence and rejoicing of God.

I am so glad that his father chose to go out to him. After you read that story, you wonder why the father did not go after the first son. One cannot chase after a rebellious person; however, you can seek for a person who is lost. So, righteousness is at the right hand of God, and what that means is right standing, right relationship.

Out of the right hand is...

- Power over the enemy, Exodus 15:6
- Salvation, Psalm 17:7
- Righteousness proceeds from the right hand, Psalm 48:10

Now let us go to the New Testament, and review some things that Jesus does. Obviously, we know that Jesus is the Son at God's right hand. He was the son of sorrow (Ben-Oni), He is the Son at God's right hand, and He is King of Kings and the Lord of Lords. Therefore purple, royalty, the amethyst, riches, wealth and all of these things belong to Him. Watch what happens in Matthew chapter 25. I find this very interesting. Beginning at verse 31, I want you to see what happens at the right hand of God.

Matthew 25:31-46 *"When the Son of man shall come in his glory, and all the holy angels with him, then shall he sit upon the throne of his glory: And before him shall be gathered all nations: and he shall separate them one from another, as a shepherd divideth his sheep from the goats: And he shall set the sheep on his right hand, but the goats on the left. Then shall the King say unto them on his right hand, Come, ye blessed of my Father, inherit the kingdom prepared for you from the foundation of the world: For I was an hunger, and ye gave me meat: I was thirsty, and ye gave me drink: I was a stranger, and ye took me in: Naked, and ye clothed me: I was sick, and ye visited me: I was in prison, and ye came unto me. Then shall the righteous answer him, saying, Lord, when saw we thee hungry, and fed thee? Or thirsty, and gave thee drink? When saw we thee a stranger, and took thee in? Or naked, and clothed thee? Or when saw we thee sick, or in prison, and came unto thee? And the King shall answer and say unto them, Verily I say unto you, Inasmuch as ye have done it unto one of the least of these my brethren, ye have done it unto me. Then shall he say also unto them on the left hand, Depart from me, ye cursed, into everlasting fire, prepared for the devil and his angels: For I was hunger, and ye gave me no meat: I was thirsty, and ye gave me no drink: I was a stranger, and ye took me not in: naked, and ye clothed me not: sick, and in prison, and ye visited me not. Then shall they also answer him, saying, Lord, when saw we thee hungry or athirst, or a stranger, or naked, or sick, or in prison, and did not minister unto thee? Then shall he answer them, saying, verily I say unto you, Inasmuch as ye did it not to one of the least of these, ye did it not to me. And these shall go away into everlasting punishment: but the righteous into life eternal."*

Everyone should highlight this passage of Scripture in their Bible. People will ask you all the time if God is good and if God is love then why does God send people to hell. Hell was never created for people. This verse could not be any clearer. Hell was created for Satan and his fallen angels. The

Lord gets no pleasure out of the death of the wicked. Jesus goes on to say, *"For I was hungry and you didn't feed me, I was thirsty and you did not give me to drink."* He is talking about the people at His left hand. Here is the point; the righteous people are at the right hand of God. In verse 33 the sheep are on the right hand and the goats are on the left hand. The sheep, the righteous enter into life eternal; but the goats, the unrighteous will go away into everlasting punishment. There is a great separation between the sheep and the goats. Given a choice, I am going to be at the right hand side of God, how about you? I am following hard after Jesus and I want nothing to do with goats. I want nothing to do with everlasting fire. I want nothing to do with hell, the devil, or torment. How wonderful to know that we are the sheep of His pasture and we are going to be divided from the goats; the sheep will go to the right and the goats will go to left.

> Mark 14:58-64 *"We heard him say, I will destroy this temple that is made with hands, and within three days I will build another made without hands. But neither so did their witness agree together. And the high priest stood up in the midst, and asked Jesus, saying, Answerest thou nothing? What is it, which these witness against thee? However, he held his peace, and answered nothing. Again, the high priest asked him, and said unto him, Art thou the Christ, the Son of the Blessed? Moreover, Jesus said, I am and ye shall see the Son of man sitting on the right hand of power, and coming in the clouds of heaven. Then the high priest rent his clothes, and saith, what need we any further witnesses? Ye have heard the blasphemy: what think ye? And they all condemned him to be guilty of death."*

In verse 58, Jesus did not say that in three days He would destroy Solomon's Temple. He was talking about the temple of His body. In three days, He would be destroyed and in three days, He would rise again. People have twisted what He said. Jesus told them in verse 62 that the right hand would be the place He would be seated and come down from Heaven. Let me put it to you this way, the position of being seated at the right hand is not here, it is in Heaven. It says you will see the Son seated in power at the right hand of God, coming in the clouds of Heaven.

> Mark 16:19-20 *"So then after the Lord had spoken unto them, he was received up into heaven, and sat on the right hand of God. And they went forth, and preached everywhere, the Lord working with them, and confirming the word with signs following."*

Another thing that he does from this position is that He gave his disciples power to perform signs and wonders. In Acts chapter 2 they were told to wait in the upper room for the Holy Spirit to come. When the feast of Pentecost came, they were all in the upper room in one accord. There were about 120 believers in prayer including Mary, the mother of Jesus, and the Holy Spirit descended. The Bible says, "there was a sound of a mighty rushing wind and tongues of fire sat on each of them." They were all in one accord and filled with the Holy Ghost speaking in other tongues as God gave them the ability. People from all of the different nations that were there for the feast of Pentecost, in the city of Jerusalem, heard them speaking in their own native languages. They just couldn't believe it and they said, aren't these guys just Galileans? How can we hear them speaking in our language? Peter got up and preached the gospel and 3000 people were saved. There's a false teaching out there that tells us that speaking in tongues was only for the beginning of the Church to get the word spread for salvation. If this teaching was true and the gift of tongues was only to start a church, then why did Peter have to get up and preach the gospel? Surely they would have heard the gospel in their native language and not have needed an additional sermon from Peter. Why did he have to get up and tell them that Jesus was the Christ whom you crucified and behold he is risen from the dead and that he grants forgiveness of sin, that Jesus is seated at the right hand and 3000 people were saved?

What they heard that day, when they heard them speaking in other tongues was men and women declaring the wonderful works of God. They heard them praising God. It is not that I suddenly get the gift of tongues and speak in German and God sends me to Germany as a missionary. That is not what this is. If that were true then what they heard was not the message of salvation Peter had to preach.

Acts 2:11 *"Cretes and Arabians, we do hear them speak in our tongues the wonderful works of God."*

Peter gives a whole gospel and if you read this chapter over a couple of times, you will see that Peter says to them, 'they denied the Christ, they denied the Holy One.' I remember reading that one day and thinking, was Peter ever forgiven, because that was the very thing he did himself, he denied Christ. The only possible way he could have preached that message was if he received forgiveness from the Lord.

Now you see Peter forgiven and standing up in front of thousands of people preaching the gospel. He said straight out that you denied the Christ. If we could all just get a hold of being forgiven, we would put the devil where he belongs so he could not use our past against us ever again. Peter was bold. I think two or three times, he accused them of denying the Lord, the very thing he had done. Now watch this, Peter is preaching the gospel to them.

> Acts 2:31-33 *"He seeing this before spake of the resurrection of Christ, that his soul was not left in hell, neither his flesh did see corruption. This Jesus hath God raised up, whereof we all are witnesses. Therefore being by the right hand of God exalted, and having received of the Father the promise of the Holy Ghost, he hath shed forth this, which ye now see and hear."*

We see that Jesus released the power of the Holy Spirit from the right hand of the Father. No one could be filled with the Spirit as we know it until He ascended into heaven to send the gift of the Father. It is not that He is just sitting at the right hand, He is really doing something. Not only is He forgiving sins and restoring people's lives, but also for those who ask, He will pour out the Holy Spirit upon them.

> Acts 5:31 *"Him hath God exalted with his right hand to be a Prince and a Saviour, for to give repentance to Israel, and forgiveness of sins."*

Not only is Jesus separating the sheep from the goats, not only is His position in heaven at the right hand, but He is also pouring out the Holy Spirit from the right hand side of God as He grants repentance and forgiveness.

> Acts 5:32 is one of my favorite verses *"And we are his witnesses of these things; and so is also the Holy Ghost, whom God hath given to them that obey him."*

Meditate on Acts chapter 5 verse 32, that God will give the Holy Spirit to those who obey him. I am convinced that the way to increase the anointing of the Holy Spirit is through obedience. When God says something, there is no argument, no debate, just do it because that will release more of the anointing of the Holy Spirit upon you. God gives the Holy Spirit to whom? To those who obey him!

Go with me to Romans 8 because there is something Jesus is actively doing for us. We have already been forgiven, correct? We have already repented. We have already received the gift of the Holy Spirit. We know we are saved. We know we are sheep. Nevertheless, there is something that Jesus is doing for us today that is found in

Romans 8:31-34 *"What shall we then say to these things? If God be for us, who can be against us? He that spared not his own Son, but delivered him up for us all, how shall he not with him also freely give us all things? Who shall lay anything to the charge of God's elect? It is God that justifies. Who is he that condemneth? It is Christ that died, yea rather, that is risen again, who is even at the right hand of God, who also maketh intercession for us."*

Then it goes on to say that, nothing can separate us from him; not stress, not persecution, and not affliction. Jesus is at the right hand of God, interceding for us. I'll be honest with you, years ago when people would say to me, please pray for me, and many times I would forget. I remember a woman asked me to pray for her son who was in a car accident. A few days later, she called me and before I could say anything to her, she started, thanking me and thanking God for all that God had done, and how my prayer for her son made all the world of difference. I had not uttered one prayer for her son. I had totally forgotten about her son completely. I could not get a word in, she just kept going on, and she was so exuberant because her son had a miraculous healing. The more she thanked me the worse I felt. Finally, I stopped her at which point I was crying and I told her that I had to repent, and that I had not prayed for her son. I felt so bad after that event, when someone says pray for me; I do it on the spot.

No matter how many good intentions we have, we forget and we have no excuse for that. Whenever anyone asks you to pray, if you can stop and pray at that moment, do it. Aren't you glad Jesus will never forget us because He's not like that, He's always at the right hand of the Father praying for us. I feel bad for Jesus because there is only one time in Scripture that I see him asking for prayer. The only place I see Jesus asking for prayer is in the garden Gethsemane. He asks his beloved disciples to stay, watch, and pray with Him. What did they do? They all fell asleep! He goes back a second time and in the Bible it says, *"He found them sleeping from sorrow."* He asked them, *"cannot they even watch and pray with Him for one hour?"* Except for that story in the Garden of Gethsemane, I do not know of any other time that he asked for prayer. When I read this verse, it moves me because He knows what we are, He knows we are but dust and we are going to fall short and miss the mark. He knows that there are nights that we are supposed to watch, pray, and yet we fall asleep. I am so glad to be able to tell you that I have a Savior who ever lives to make intercessions for me. That even right now, at the right hand of God, He is praying for us. If I can get a prayer answered and you can get a prayer answered, what do you think happens when Jesus prays? There is no verse in the Bible that I am aware of where His prayers went unanswered. He is the Benjamin, the son of the right-hand. Of all the sons of Jacob, Benjamin was the only son born in the Promised Land.

The only time in the whole Bible that I could find Jesus standing at the right-hand is when they stoned Stephen. This is found in Acts chapter 7 where they murdered a young deacon named of Stephen. As they stoned Stephen he said, *"Lord, lay not this sin to their charge."* 'Forgive them.' Then the Scripture says that the heavens opened and Stephen said, *"I see the glory of God and Jesus standing at the right hand of the father."* The Spirit of God spoke to me and said, every time you forgive someone who has hurt you, I am going to stand up for you. Wow thank You Jesus, may we stand up for You as You are standing up for us.

Before I close this chapter, I want to mention the blessing from Jacob in the book of Genesis.

Genesis 49:27 *"Benjamin shall raven as a wolf: In the morning, he shall devour the prey, and at night, he shall divide the spoil."*

Benjamin was to devour the prey and divide the spoil that is exactly what Jesus has done for us.

I want to show you also the blessing from Moses in Deuteronomy.

Deuteronomy 33:12 *"And of Benjamin he said, the beloved of the Lord shall dwell in safety by him: and the Lord shall cover him all the day long, and he shall dwell between his shoulders."*

How thankful I am for the Lords love and that we dwell with Him in safety, and He covers us and we dwell close to His heart between his shoulders.

## Closing Prayer

*Lord Jesus, I thank You that You were Benoni, the Son of Sorrows, a man familiar with grief. That you became the Son of God seated at the right hand, exalted to majesty on high. You certainly deserve the amethyst stone of royalty, for you are my King of Kings, Lord of Lords. Lord, I just thank You that from the right hand of God You have forgiven my sins. You have purged me. You have poured out the gift of the Holy Spirit upon me. You speak to me from the right hand and Lord I know that there is going to be a day that I will be at the right hand with You and You will welcome me to the kingdom that your Father prepared for me. You will one day separate the sheep from the goats and the goats will depart into everlasting fire. Lord I just want to thank you for being my Prince and Savior. I want to thank You that whenever I have to forgive someone, You stand up for me at the right hand of the Father empowering me and enabling me to do the same. I thank You for the stone of the amethyst, from the tribe of Benjamin, the son of my right hand. I ask that you continue to bless my time with You as You continue to open the Scriptures to me. I ask You to open my ears to hear what the Spirit is saying, in Jesus name, Amen.*

# CHAPTER 11

## – The Tenth Stone –
## The Beryl of Dan

*Father, we come to You with thankful hearts for Your awesome Word. And we know that Your Word is settled in heaven. Heavenly Father, open the eyes of our hearts as we begin to look at the tenth stone in the breastplate of the high priest. Give us the supernatural ability to apply this truth to our lives, because we are a royal priesthood, and we are living stones. And so Lord, thank You for this revelation knowledge and for the Holy Spirit who leads and guides us into all truth. In Jesus name. Amen.*

Genesis 30:1-6 *"Now when Rachel saw that she bore Jacob no children, Rachel envied her sister, and said to Jacob, "Give me children, or else I die!" And Jacob's anger was aroused against Rachel, and he said, "Am I in the place of God, who has withheld from you the fruit of the womb?" So she said, "Here is my maid Bilhah; go in to her, and she will bear a child on my knees, that I also may have children by her." Then she gave him Bilhah her maid as wife, and Jacob went in to her. And Bilhah conceived and bore Jacob a son. Then Rachel said, 'God has judged my case; and He has also heard my voice and given me a son.' Therefore, she called his name Dan."*

Here is Rachel who has bitterness in her heart; she is jealous and envious of Leah who already has had four sons: Ruben, Simeon, Levi and Judah. Once Leah started to praise God, her life changed for the better; however, Rachel's life changed for the worse because she harbored bitterness in her heart. Rachel decided to give Jacob her handmaiden Bilhah. The first child this handmaiden conceived was a son who Rachel named *Dan*, as seen in verse six. This means, 'God has judged me.'

The Key Definition for *Dan* is "to be judged or to be a judge." It is really a shame that Rachel was in such competition with her sister Leah.

Sometimes when you meet someone, there is just something about them that you really do not care for; they have an air about them or there is something about them that causes you to make a quick judgment. I remember years ago I met a woman whom I did not like the moment I met her. She had an ostentatious  air about her. She exuded wealth (not that there is anything wrong with being rich.) Her appearance was flawless and her clothing was all coordinated. Her shoes matched the hat, the hat matched the purse, and of course, everything matched the coat. She drove a brand new Lincoln with leather seats. I thought to myself, 'I don't want to have anything to do with her.' I really did not care for her. She started to regularly attend one of the Bible studies that I was teaching. Through the grapevine she heard how much I love coffee.

One day, my doorbell rings, there on my front porch stands the woman with a pound of Dunkin' Donuts coffee. Now what was I supposed to do? I wanted to accept the coffee, but I could not just shut the door in her face. Therefore, I said, "Come on in and I'll make some coffee." Then I sat down with her and suspended my preconceived judgment based on what she appeared to be like. We ended up with a very deep and long lasting friendship that we still have to this day. As I got past the appearance of things, I learned that she had some heartache in her life. She relied on material things to give her some sense of security. Her husband was verbally abusive to her, and thee material comforts took the edge off the pain. She ended up becoming ill, and her husband did not show love or support for her even though they had been married for years. Since she could not be intimate with him, he cheated on her. She finally got the courage to separate from him. I tell you this not because of how she suffered or because of how wrongly she was treated, but because of how I had so misjudged her.

We are going to look at what it means to judge. Who are we to judge, how are we to judge, and what does Jesus say about judging? We are to judge those who are within the faith. In other words, we are to judge believers, not those outside of the faith, because God will take care of the nonbelievers.

> 1 Corinthians 5:11-13 *"But now I have written to you not to keep company with anyone named a brother, who is sexually immoral, or covetous, or an idolater, or a reviler, or a drunkard, or an extortioner not even to eat with such a person. For what have I to do with judging those also who are outside? Do you not judge those who are inside? But those who are outside God judges. Therefore, "put away from yourselves the evil person."*

Beginning with verse 11; now this is a little tough, but it is saying 'if there is a brother or sister in the faith who tells me they love the Lord, yet I know for certain that they are practicing wicked sin deliberately, I cannot and should not eat with such a person.' I have to judge that sin in their life and hope that they come to repentance. It actually says 'if you have a brother who is having sexual relations outside marriage, or who is stealing or an adulterer, do not even eat with such a brother.'

I have had to make use of this Scripture only once in all the years. I went to lunch with a woman once, and while at lunch, the Spirit of the Lord spoke to me while I was at the salad bar. He dropped the word of knowledge within my heart. The Lord said to me 'she was involved with a married man and that He wanted me to rebuke her.' Well, I started to chew like briar rabbit. The last thing I wanted to do was to look over my salad and tell this woman what the Lord had revealed. Therefore, I looked at her and said that I sense that the Lord is showing me that you are in sexual sin. She looked at me and her eyes got huge, as they filled with tears, she bowed her head. Afterwards, we went out to my car. She confessed that she had been involved with a married man for three years, and that yes, she was committing adultery. We had a time of prayer and I prayed that she would have the strength to break that relationship.

About a month went by and she called and asked me to go to lunch with her. The minute we began to talk, the verse 1Corinthians chapter 5 verse 12 came to mind *"with such a one don't even eat."* I asked her "if she had broken all ties with this ungodly relationship." She responded, "I have not." Therefore, I told her I could not eat with her until she repented. I hung up the phone and began to cry, because I do not like to hurt people. However,

I had to obey the word of God. I had to make a judgment on this. It is not as if she had not had time to repent and straighten out this matter before God. If I had gone to lunch with her, I would have been in sin. I did not want to be disobedient to what God was saying and what I knew was the right thing to do. Later on when she called me after she broke up with him, I was happy to have lunch with her. She ended up marrying someone else, and is in a wonderful ministry today. You cannot read a verse like this and just overlook it. Now I am not telling you, to nit-pick, or to look for sin in everybody else's life, because, we have enough challenges of our own. The Bible makes it very clear that you are to judge those who are believers.

It also depends on how we judge. Additional Scriptures, one in the Old Testament and the other in the New Testament will show us some helpful guidelines when it comes to judging. From the Old Testament we are going to look at Isaiah. We have established that the name *Dan* means "to judge or to be judged." His stone is the beryl. The Key Definition for *beryl* means, "to break and subdue."

> Isaiah 11:1-3 *"And there shall come forth a rod out of the stem of Jesse, and a Branch shall grow out of his roots: And the spirit of the LORD shall rest upon him, the spirit of wisdom and understanding, the spirit of counsel and might, the spirit of knowledge and of the fear of the LORD; And shall make him of quick understanding in the fear of the LORD: and he shall not judge after the sight of his eyes, neither reprove after the hearing of his ears: But with righteousness shall he judge the poor, and reprove with equity for the meek of the earth: and he shall smite the earth: with the rod of his mouth, and with the breath of his lips shall he slay the wicked."*

From verse 3 we see that Jesus does not judge by what He sees, or what He hears. Aren't you glad that when it comes to being judged, Jesus reads your heart and not just your actions? What if Jesus judged us by our behavior? We would all be in trouble but He looks beyond what it seems like and beyond our words because He reads our hearts. We do not have the ability to do that with someone else's heart. Therefore, when it comes to making a judgment, please pray this verse: 'God would make you of a quick understanding and that you would have counsel in wisdom and the fear of the Lord. And that you would judge not by the seeing of your eyes or the hearing of your ears, but with a right spirit and in righteousness would you judge.' The only reason I had to do that hard thing years ago, was that

God wanted her to come back to Him wholeheartedly. God wanted her to be free of something the enemy had set up as a snare in her life.

Jesus even talked about this in John chapter 7. Isn't it sad that sometimes we have to learn the hard way? However, you know that once you learn something the hard way, you never forget it. Moreover, because I have done this and made the mistake of prejudging, or judging by appearance, I am very careful now to avoid this pitfall. In John 7, Jesus is speaking; if you look at verse 24, it could not be any clearer. He says, *"Judge not according to the appearance, but judge righteous judgment."* Do you see it? Don't judge by appearance. Judgment should be made with the help of the Spirit and not by what it looks like. I heard an analogy sometime ago which I thought was good. Let us say for instance that I left my jacket inside, and when I went outside it was raining. Then I said to my friend, "run back into the church and grab my jacket for me." Now no one saw me speak to her outside. She runs in and grabs my leather jacket, and out the door she goes. If you were going to judge by what you saw, it would look like she took my coat, right?

I remember one time one of our elders of our church had a dog who had digested anti-freeze. Now anti-freeze is poisonous to a dog. It was a Sunday afternoon and they had to call the poison control center. The poison control told them "if you want to save your dog, you need to get some 140 proof whiskey into the dog and by taking this action there would be a good chance of recovery. So our elder went to the liquor store to purchase the whiskey he needed for his dog. The next thing you know, I got a telephone call and a report that our elder was seen on a Sunday afternoon going into a liquor store. I called him and requested a meeting that night. My husband and I went over and found out what actually happened. How do you think I felt when I found out the truth? This was a misjudgment on everyone's part because we were too quick to judge. I was too quick to call a meeting without fully understanding the story, along with having all of the facts prior to passing judgment.

Matthew 7:1-5 *"Judge not, that ye be not judged. For with what judgment ye judge, ye shall be judged: and with what measure ye mete, it shall be measured to you again. Why beholdest thou the mote that is in thy brother's eye, but considerest not the beam that is in thine own eye? On the other hand, how wilt thou say to thy brother, Let me pull out the mote out of thine eye; and, behold, a beam is in thine own eye. Thou hypocrite, first cast out the beam out of thine own eye; and then shalt thou see clearly to cast out the mote out of thy brother's eye."*

What have we established? Who do we have to judge? Believers who are not living in a godly manner are the ones that are to be judged. Jesus tells us in Matthew chapter 7, 'we are to be slow to judge and He will be slow to judge us.' If I am kind to you, He will send kindness into my life. We do reap what we have sown. Jesus is saying to us with the same measure we judge people that same level of judgment will return to us. This will help us slow down before you make a judgment. He continues in the verse 3 by saying, "Why beholdest thou the mote that is in thy brother's eye, but considerest not the beam that is in thine own eye?"

Here is how I interrupted the above Scripture; 'say I have a huge baseball bat sticking out of my eye and I see a toothpick in your eye I would say, you better take that toothpick out, because it can hurt your vision. Jesus would say, why would you nit-pick over a toothpick in somebody else's eye when you are blind as a bat because you have not judged your own life?'

(NIV) Matthew 7:3-5 *"Why do you look at the speck of sawdust in your brother's eye and pay no attention to the plank in your own eye? How can you say to your brother, 'Let me take the speck out of your eye,' when all the time there is a plank in your own eye? You hypocrite, first take the plank out of your own eye, and then you will see clearly to remove the speck from your brother's eye."*

You know what this says to me, you had better make sure you see clearly. Before I find all the sawdust in your life, and I had better make sure all of the wood is out of my life. Remember that the measure I gave to you God will give back to me. I desire mercy, so I choose to be merciful to you. Remember to make sure that you take care of your own planks and beams before you go on the sawdust trail.

I was brought up a devout Catholic. One of the things the Roman Catholic Church taught me is that you always have to have a time of confession, or pray at the end of your day the Act of Contrition.

1 Corinthians 11:31-32 *"For if we would judge ourselves, we should not be judged. But when we are judged, we are chastened of the Lord, that we should not be condemned with the world."*

The most important judgment I can make is my own self-examination. No one can read another person's heart. Instead of being busy judging others and getting into their business, the wisest thing I can do is judge myself and do it according to the Word of God.

2 Corinthians 10:11-13 *"Let such a one think this, that, such as we are in word by letters when we are absent, such will we be also in deed when we are present. For we dare not make ourselves of the number, or compare ourselves with some that commend themselves: but they (who are) measuring themselves by themselves, and comparing themselves among themselves, are not wise. But we will not boast of things without our measure, but according to the measure of the rule which God hath distributed to us, a measure to reach even unto you."*

Simply put, he who compares himself with himself is not wise. To judge would be another word for compare. So many times, we examine ourselves against others. We can look good against someone else, but Jesus is our standard, and compared to him we would all fall short. Rarely do we judge ourselves by someone who is our equal. Therefore, if you want to judge yourself against anyone, it would be Jesus. We have a personal walk with God, and we have to keep open communication with the Lord daily. Judge ourselves right away according to the written Word of God.

Dan needed to be judged, because this tribe introduced idolatry to the children of Israel. The children of Dan set up graven images. One of the things that we have to watch out for is that there is no serpent in the way; that we do not have any idols or idolatry in our lives.

I always thought of idolatry in relation to the worship of a statue. Then I came to realize that anything that we put above God is an idol. Many years ago right after my son had become spirit filled; he was really living for the Lord. He was fasting and praying and I was so very proud of him. One particular Sunday, I was getting ready to go to communion and as I was walking up the aisle, the Lord said. "You're not worthy to eat at my table today." What a shock that was to me! Because, I was not aware any sin in my life at that time. I asked the Lord "I can't have communion today?" The Lord said, "You have an idol." I had already cleared out all of the symbols of Catholicism from my house many years ago, that is why His statement shocked me so. I was getting ready to argue with the Lord when He spoke again and said, "it is your son." I began to realize that I had put my son above the place where the Lord belonged. I had forgotten that my son was a sinner, saved by grace, and that he could miss the mark. He was simply a human being. Gradually I had let this sanctified, spirit filled, godly young man become like an idol in my heart. There was a time when he was about eight years old, and the neighborhood kids were cursing outside. My son came home, saying to me, "Mom, I'm not going to be around that." The kids were making fun of him and were calling him names from across the street, and they were mocking him. It was summer time and the screen door was open. I heard the kids jeering, "you don't have any friends, no one's going to play with you, you are such a Jesus Sissy." My son walked out on the front porch and said, "what friend of yours gives eternal life?" All of the kids scattered. The thoughts that ran through my head were, 'Wow what friend of yours can give you eternal life' this was a bold step for such a young child.

So, for that particular Sunday, I did not take communion because I knew I wasn't ready yet to dethrone my son. I had to realize that ultimately he was not my son; he was God's son first. I had to see that my daughter was just as important to me as he was, and that they were both even more important to God. After some examination, I realized that I was putting too much emphasis on my son and that I was favoring him. I asked God to forgive me and was able to take communion the next Sunday. The point is that we always think of idols as worshiping voodoo dolls, biting off a chicken's head, hanging a horseshoe above the door, or wearing a horn around your neck.

An idol is anything that we put above the Lord. Do you know what Americans number one idol is? It could be sports or fame; however, it might very well be 'almighty dollar?' Why does every single tournament and event have to be on Sunday morning at 10 o'clock? Soccer, football, and the majority of sporting events are going to conflict with our church service. Do you know why that is? The devil wants to get the young kids, especially the boys, out of church so that they do not come into manhood and serve God with their lives.

When my children were young, we told them that there is nothing before God's house, absolutely nothing! That meant no sports played on Sundays during church hours. When my son and my daughter were active in sports, they would tell the coach that they would not be there any Sunday until after 12 o'clock. Many times, we would go to church with their uniforms in the trunk. After church, they would run and get dressed their uniforms on and away we would go to the field.

Since we have seen the correct way to judge, Dan can now prepare to receive the blessing from Jacob.

Genesis 49:16-17 *"Dan shall judge his people, as one of the tribes of Israel. Dan shall be a serpent by the way, an adder in the path, that biteth the horse heels, so that his rider shall fall backward."*

This is a very complex text, and I do not have all the insight on it that I would like. As far as all the stones we have looked at, everything has been very positive. In addition, I have tried my best to give you the upside of each stone and there tribe. However, in this verse there is a warning that we should all heed.

There are three things; I want to show you about the serpent's way. We have to make sure that we hold onto the reins of the horse and that the serpent is not able to knock us down.

Judges 18:30-31 *"And the children of Dan set up the graven image: and Jonathan, the son of Gershom, the son of Manasseh, he and his sons were priests to the tribe of Dan until the day of the captivity of the land. And they set them up Micah's graven image, which he made, all the time that the house of God was in Shiloh."*

The children of Dan enticed the beginning stages of the tribe to enter into idolatry. Watch what happen in 1 Kings 12 as it gets far worse. There is an infamous king named Jeroboam, and he practiced blatant sin and idolatry. First, he decided that he would put his best friends in the priesthood, even though they were not Levites. This was an abomination before God, he did some very wicked things.

*1 Kings 12:26-33 "And Jeroboam said in his heart, Now shall the kingdom return to the house of David: If this people go up to do sacrifice in the house of the LORD at Jerusalem, then shall the heart of this people turn again unto their lord, even unto Rehoboam king of Judah, and they shall kill me, and go again to Rehoboam king of Judah. Whereupon the king took counsel, and made two calves of gold, and said unto them, It is too much for you to go up to Jerusalem: behold thy gods, O Israel, which brought thee up out of the land of Egypt. And he set the one in Bethel, and the other put he in Dan. And this thing became a sin: for the people went to worship before the one, even unto Dan. And he made an house of high places, and made priests of the lowest of the people, which were not of the sons of Levi. And Jeroboam ordained a feast in the eighth month, on the fifteenth day of the month, like unto the feast that is in Judah , and he offered upon the altar. So did he in Bethel, Sacrificing unto the calves that he had made: one he placed in Bethel the other was placed in Dan. So he offered upon the altar which he had made in Bethel the fifteenth day of the eighth month, even in the month which he had devised of his own heart; and ordained a feast unto the children of Israel: and he offered upon the altar, and burnt incense."*

King Jeroboam is worried that if they went up to Jerusalem to worship God they would follow king Rehoboam, who was a righteous king. Instead of the people going to Jerusalem meaning 'one who possesses peace' to worship, they worshipped the golden calf in the city of Dan as well as the city of Bethel.

Amos 8:14 *"They that swear by the sin of Samaria, and say, Thy god, O Dan, liveth; and, the manner of Beersheba liveth; even they shall fall, and never rise up again."*

This particular place in Samaria where the Bible says "thy god, O Dan, liveth" actually became the center of idol worship and a hindrance in the progress of God's children. They continued to worship the golden calves in this city of Dan.

I am glad to be able to share with you a blessing that Moses spoke over Dan.

Deuteronomy 33:22 *"And of Dan he said, Dan is a lion's whelp: he shall leap from Bashan.*"

First of all the definition of a lion's whelp is 'a young baby lion.' Let me show you a couple of things that the Bible says about a young lion. If you had the choice of being a serpent in the way, or a young lion, which would you be? A young lion of course!

Ezekiel 19:1-3 *"Moreover take thou up a lamentation for the princes of Israel, And say, what is thy mother? A lioness: she lay down among lions; she nourished her whelps among young lions. And she brought up one of her whelps: it became a young lion, and it learned to catch the prey; it devoured men."*

With good teaching from the lioness, the young lions will learn to catch prey and defend themselves. We can actually become like young lions to succeed against the enemy. In verse 3, it states that young lion has been properly trained so it will be able to catch the prey, destroy, and devour it. I want to be like this young lion with the Lion of the tribe of Judah so that no matter what serpent is in the way, or, no matter what's trying to bite me at the heel, Jesus will help me to rise above it. The lioness trains the lion's whelp, as the female lion does all of the hunting. We have all seen large lions that lay around all day inactive occasionally let out a roar. However, it is the female lioness; that is on guard, moving through the reeds and going after the prey.

Deuteronomy 33:22 *"And of Dan he said, Dan is a lion's whelp: he shall leap from Bashan."*

The definition for a *Bashan* is "to be fruitful." God wants us to produce fruit for His kingdom and the enemy tries to deter us, as young trained lions we can increase in our production for God and His kingdom.

I have said little on the stone of Dan, which is the beryl stone. The word beryl as mentioned before means, 'to subdue.' I looked up the word subdue for a fuller understanding of this stone and found that subdue means to restrain, hold back, or bring somebody under forcible control. Jesus has subdued the enemy and our prayer is that as we submit to God, He will restrain and hold back every advance made against us. Before I close this chapter please look with at Daniel where he has a vision of Jesus and beryl is mentioned in this verse.

> Daniel 10: 5-6 *"Then I lifted up mine eyes, and looked, and behold a certain man clothed in linen, whose loins [were] girded with fine gold of Uphaz: His body also [was] like the beryl, and his face as the appearance of lightning, and his eyes as lamps of fire, and his arms and his feet like in colour to polished brass, and the voice of his words like the voice of a multitude."*

## Key Point

Remember… judge yourself, lest you be judged. Judging yourself is your first line of defense. Judging yourself will protect you from falling back. Then as a young lion trained by God, you can to go after the enemy.

Remember… find out what God's Word says about you. Speak the Word of God and declare it so that when the serpent tries to bite, you will not fall backwards.

Remember…Jesus has destroyed all the work of the enemy.

## Closing Prayer

*Father, want to thank You for the stone of beryl, which means to subdue. Lord, I want the serpent to be subdued and out of my life. I know, Father, that I have to be careful not to pass judgment or criticize anyone. Your Word tells me so clearly not to worry about a speck in someone else's eye, when I cannot even see where I am going due to the plank in my own eye. Would You please help me to judge myself according to Your Word. And Lord, when I need to make a judgment, let it be by the Spirit of God. In Isaiah it says that you made him have a quick understanding, that he judged not by the seeing of his eye or the hearing of his ears; but with righteousness he passes judgment. Lord, please teach me to judge righteously, not by what I think, or what I see or hear, but with a right heart. Lord, I pray that just as a young lion, You would teach me to catch the prey. When the serpent is in the way, let me not fall back. Lord, I am standing on Psalm 91 and trust You that no harm or injury will come to me because I abide under the shadow of the Almighty. I have made You my refuge and my hope. In Jesus name, Amen.*

# CHAPTER 12

# – The Eleventh Stone –
# The Onyx of Asher

*Father, I thank You for the Word of God and I thank You that through Your Spirit you have opened to us the deeper things of God. Lord, I believe that through these lessons and chapters, we have actually partaken of hidden manna. Lord, we have learned things that we never could have understood before except by your Spirit. We are so thankful for your Son, Jesus. We are so thankful that we are living stones and that Jesus carries us over His heart, just like the high priest with the twelve stones of beauty and glory. As we begin this chapter, we ask You to visit us with your Holy Spirit, with truth and revelation, so that we would grow to be more like You, Lord. We do not only need head knowledge, we need our hearts changed so it can affect us every day of our lives. We thank you now in Jesus Name, Amen.*

I would like to do a quick overview of the rows of stones in the breastplate of the high priest and then we will get into this chapter of study.

**1st Row**

The Sardius: Judah

- ◆ Because of the blood of Jesus we can give praise to God

The Topaz: Issachar

- ◆ You are rewarded for service

The Carbuncle: Zebulun

- ◆ We dwell in the light

## 2nd Row

The Emerald: Reuben

- ◆ Throne of the First Born were we will see Jesus;
  this is the Covenant of Promise

The Sapphire: Simeon

- ◆ God has heard me and is polishing me through affliction

The Diamond: Gad

- ◆ We are more than conquerors through the crown of Jesus,
  the Great Lion who crushed Satan

## 3rd Row

The Ligure: Ephraim

- ◆ Doubly fruitful in affliction yields a double portion of joy

The Agate: Manasseh

- ◆ Causing me to forget the pain of my past
  and pressing on toward the high calling

The Amethyst: Benjamin

- ◆ Jesus is seated at the right hand of the Father
  and one day will welcome me

## 4th Row

The Beryl: Dan

- ◆ Subdue the serpent by making a right judgment

Genesis 30:13 *"And Leah said, Happy am I, for the daughters will call me blessed: and she called his name Asher."*

The Key Definition for *Asher* is "happy." I have said this before, but do not mind repeating that happiness and joy are two different things. Joy is the product of the Holy Spirit within us. We can be joyful even in the midst of a painful, hurtful event. Happiness depends on what is happening in the natural. Leah named her child "happy" because things had turned around in her life. Also, in the end we see that Leah considered herself fortunate and happy.

Genesis 49:20 *"Out of Asher his bread shall be fat, and he shall yield royal dainties."*

I am very excited because the tribe of Asher has a very well known, prominent woman in the New Testament. In the book of Acts, Paul might have referred to the fact he was from the tribe of Benjamin but overall, you do not really see the tribes mentioned throughout the New Testament. Later on in this chapter, we are going to take a good look at one of the instrumental women in the book of Acts. It actually says she was from the tribe of Asher.

When you look at the first portion of this Scripture it says, "his bread shall be fat." This can be interpreted to mean that he has rich food or rich bread. The term *fat* in the Bible is defined as "everything you need" or in other words, "prosperous." Later on, you are going to see that the onyx stone actually has something to do with manna, which is the bread of God. Therefore, the blessing Jacob gives to this happy son is that he is going to have a supply of bread. Since we do not live in the Middle East and because we do not have bread as a main staple, we don't understand how important this was to them. One of the greatest blessings you could tell someone in that day was that they would always have bread.

I was speaking with my son and his family recently when he had just purchased a loaf of garlic bread. I said, "My father would never allow bread on the table." Now that I have had time to look back, I understand that because my mom and dad went through the Great Depression, my father had to stand in line for hours for a piece of bread and a cup of soup. Once the Depression was over, my father got a good job. He said that there would never be bread on his table because it was a poor man's food. We were never allowed to have bread with our meals either. Because of this, even after all these years, I never think to buy rolls or put bread on the table. As they say, you are a product of your environment. I remember one time when my grandson Jacob was little and we had Thanksgiving dinner together. There was turkey, creamed onions, stuffing, mashed potatoes, etc.; it was simply marvelous. And here was Jacob, who couldn't have been more than two and half years old, sitting in his high chair, looking up and saying, "What, no bread?" I mean, he had his hands in the air and it was as if none of this was important unless we had bread.

I am simply uninterested in bread and if I never eat another piece of it again it would not bother me. Someone else could live on bread alone. When my husband was a boy, his mother would make loaves of Italian bread. She would make three or four loaves of bread at a time. Then she would get the bread hot from the oven, and then each of her children would get a loaf of bread, a stick of butter, and eat the bread hot. Therefore, you understand my husband really loves bread, all kinds, and varieties.

The point is that Asher was promised in God's Word, "Man shall not live by bread alone, but on every word that proceeds out of the mouth of God." We must understand how important it is to get into the word of God. We need the manna of life; we need the bread of life. We need that manna, the fresh bread of God. That is the kind of bread that I choose and prefer to eat everyday. I am into the bread of the Word. Asher is promised things, rich food, or bread, and this is food that they would serve royalty or dignitaries. In other versions, it might say, "his food would be fit for kings." Imagine you go to the day old bread store and there is nothing wrong with that, especially when the cost of bread is astronomical, but when bread has been there a week and you eat it, it is stale and you are extremely disappointed. When I look at this I say "God, I want fresh manna, right out of the oven of heaven, so fresh it's hot to touch!" He was promised plenty of bread, which was their main staple, and he was promised that the bread he would have would be good enough to set before kings.

Deuteronomy 33:24-25 *"And of Asher he said, Let Asher be blessed with children; let him be acceptable to his brethren, and let him dip his foot in oil. Thy shoes shall be iron and brass; and as thy days, so shall thy strength be."*

In Deuteronomy chapter 33, Moses had a lot to say about Asher. Again, all these tribes are different and all the stones are different. Some of them have a long blessing from Jacob, and not a word from Moses. Just like in the previous Scripture, there was one verse from Jacob with a blessing of an abundance of bread. You are going to see that Moses blessings for the tribe of Asher are detail. In fact, there are five things; I would like to show you in the Scripture. Remember God has not only just given us joy, He wants us to be happy and He wants to give us fresh bread. He wants us to eat with Him because He is the King. Let us face it when Jesus feeds you fresh bread you are not dining alone. Rarely have you walked into a restaurant and seen a table for one! I know that I do not like to eat alone; I would rather sit and eat with the King!

We see in the initial portion of verse 24 that Asher is going to be blessed with children. Looking back over the previous chapters, I do not remember any of the other tribes being blessed with children. Many of them had children, but it is interesting that he said to Asher that, *"he would be blessed with children."* By the way, the children here could mean spiritual children. If you have ever led someone to the Lord or discipled them, they would be considered your spiritual children. Later on God may remove them and say listen, they need to grow up because they are too dependent on you. You need to let them go. I remember when I first was saved; my mentor became everything to me. Every day we would read Scripture and pray together. However, after several years I began to call her instead of praying about things myself. I mean, I would never even think to ask God first. There was a time in my life when God said to me; "just cut it off." We are still friends and we still see each other, but I came to realize how easy it is for spiritual children to become dependent on the one who brings them into salvation. It is easy for the spiritual child to hang on but they have to learn how to hear from God themselves and seek first the kingdom of God. To those of you who might mentor, or lead people to the Lord, just realize that there will come a time where you have to wean them. Just as a baby does not like it, I did not like it.

In the second part of verse 24, we see that Asher is going to be accepted by his brothers. In other words, you are going to have family acceptance. In verse 25 we see, *"thy shoes shall be iron and brass"* so not only did he have a nice pedicure because his feet were rubbed in oil, but the shoes that he put on were made of iron and brass.

The blessing that Moses gave Asher is that he would be extremely strong.

First, Blessed with children…

Do you know that children are supposed to be a blessing from God?

Moreover, all of us who have children say "Amen." However, there are seasons where we do not feel so blessed. You have to read Psalm 127 where it speaks of children being a heritage of the Lord and blessed is the man whose quiver is full. I had two children and that was enough for me. I remember times when I had challenges with my "blessings" and I would just have to quote Scriptures and speak promises. I would allow them to get away with many things. My children turned out well because my husband was a good disciplinarian. He was great at setting boundaries and giving an appropriate punishment. I mean, he simply amazed me. One time my son and one of his friends found out that the boy next door was having a birthday party. My son and his friend filled water balloons, threw them over the fence, and bombed all these little kids at the party. The kids at the party were screaming and crying, so my neighbor came over to discuss the situation with me. I asked her to wait until my husband came home. When I told my husband, what had happened, my husband's punishment for my son was our son to go over and apologize to the neighbor, and then for the next three months, he had to cut the neighbors grass and carry out their trash. That is exactly what our son did for the entire summer. Every couple of weeks our neighbor would tell him, "that's enough; you don't have to do this anymore. Our son responded each time by telling him that he had to do what his father asked him to do.

In another instance, we found out that our daughter was smoking. No matter what we said or did, we could not get her to stop. We could stop her from smoking inside the house but we could not stop her from smoking when she was not at home. I was not going to fall for the same line that I gave my parents, "Mom if you just let me smoke in front of you, I'll smoke less." Who would ever believe that one? Well, my parents let me start smoking in the house at the age of 15, and it became an addiction and struggle for years to come. So when I found cigarettes in my daughter's room and started smelling smoke around the house, we had a big "discussion" about it. "You're not smoking in this house, not until you're 18, even then you're going to smoke on the porch outside." Mind you, this was even before it was socially unacceptable to smoke cigarettes. One time I was up in her room straightening up and I happened to find a pack of cigarettes in a snow boot in the back of her closet. Suddenly this Scripture came to mind, *"rebellion is bound up in the heart of a child but the rod of correction will drive it from them."* I did not know exactly what to do with that, but that was the Scripture the Lord gave me. I believed that the Lord was telling me that I needed to spank her with a belt, but I had never really disciplined her biblically before. My husband came home from work that evening and after we finished eating dinner, while we were all still sitting at the table, I said to my husband, "by the way, would you take off your belt?" He asked me why I wanted him to take his belt off and I said, "Because I have to administer discipline to our daughter." Now my daughter was about fifteen years old, one might say that she was a bit too old to be spanked with a belt. However, I had to do what the Lord said to do. I gave her the cigarettes I had found and then I recited the Scripture verse, *"rebellion is bound up in the heart, and the rod of correction will drive it from you."* Then I said, "Go into the living room I am going to take a belt to you and drive out the rebellion from your heart." My daughter goes into the living room, and I am literally shaking. I go into the living room, and mind you, she had jeans on, so I did not abuse her. I hit her once with the belt and nothing happened. I decided to hit her until she cried or I cried, whichever came first. I continued giving her a few slaps and she started sobbing. Now listen to this, I did not hurt her, there was not a mark on her. She had heavy jeans on and I am not very strong. She started sobbing and said, "thank you" and then I started crying and said, "You're welcome." She was crying and went up the stairs saying, 'thank you.' (This is the God's honest truth, you could ask her or my husband) and I was in the living room sobbing, 'you're welcome, you're welcome.' I have to tell you, today she does not smoke. I realize when God tells you to do something, you have to do it. You have to obey God. I used to have to tell my daughter continually that she was a blessing and I made this declaration consistently over my children. I did discipline my blessing. I want to encourage you, parents, and grandparents, especially when you see your children or children's children being drawn into temptation, because there are many temptations out there and the morals have totally decayed in our society today. Search the Bible for Scriptures and start quoting them over your children. I have certain promises I am holding onto for my daughter. God gave me a promise in the book of Ezekiel; like mother, like daughter. She loves the Lord and I believe I am actually one day going to see her preach the Word of God before I die. So find the promises and read Psalm 127.

Secondly, He is accepted by his brothers...

How awesome it is to grow up in a house were you are accepted just for who you are? I mean everyone wants to be accepted. I looked at Asher and I thought, you are accepted by the brothers. Then I thought, if Asher ever talked to Joseph again one day, how their stories would differ. Asher was accepted by all his brothers. Every one of us needs acceptance. One of the verses that helped me along the way is Psalm chapter 27 verse 10 which says: *"If my mother or my father rejects me, God receives me."* I cannot tell you how many times I needed that verse.

When I became a born again Christian my own family did not accept my faith. I was excommunicated because I "changed my religion." I remember when my mother, who was the youngest of nine brothers and sisters, died, not one of her other relatives came to the funeral. Not one aunt, uncle, cousin, or niece. I started receiving letters that said I was going to burn in hell for not burying her in a certain denomination. For a couple of years I used to send Christmas cards to my family members. They would send them back unopened, stamped 'return to sender.' By about the third year, I thought, you know I have had enough of this, I do not deserve this kind of treatment. I did what my mother asked me to do. I do not owe them an explanation and if they do not want to have anything to do with me, then so be it. I cannot help but tell you how bad it hurts at times. I had a huge family. I have not seen or talked to them since my dad died and I called my Uncle and said, "Uncle Ralph, my daddy died tonight." My uncle said, "Did you bury him like a heathen too?" I said goodbye to my uncle and have not spoken with him since 1979. Therefore, going through life I realized that God accepts me and loves me. I am accepted by the body of believers and have a truly great family.

Third, His feet will be covered in oil...

This means that God anointed his steps. In the book of Luke, it describes the woman who began to wash Jesus' feet with her tears and anointed them with fragrant oil. The Pharisee of the house said, *"if He knew who this woman was, He wouldn't let her touch him."* Jesus told the woman that her sins were forgiven and then turned to the Pharisee and said, "I came into your house and you gave me no kiss. And you gave me no water to wash my feet, but this woman has washed my feet with her tears and anointed them with oil." In the book of Leviticus, did you know that the priest would take anointing oil and the blood then he would anoint the right ear lobe, the right thumb, and the big toe on the right foot for a trespass offering? If you and I could get this anointing; on what we hear, what we put our hand to, or where we go it would save us a lot of trouble.

Fourth, Shoes of iron and brass...

Brass in the Bible speaks of judgment and iron and was used to make weapons along with common tools. It is also a symbol of a ruling power, as you see in Revelation chapter 19 verse 20 it says 'Jesus will return with a rod of iron to judge the nations.' The definition of *iron* in some Scriptures is "fear." I thought maybe, God gives him judgment or brass over the fear or iron in his life. When we consider the armor of God, we talk about our feet being shod with the preparation of peace. Brass and iron are heavy. I remember as a young person, because I am of Dutch origin, I would put on my grandparents wooden shoes and walk around in them. I would have to be very careful and watch how I walked because they were not normal shoes even though they were very comfortable. After reading this verse I thought, wouldn't it do us all a world of good to get some brass and iron on our feet to make us slow down just a little bit and be careful of our steps. Could not we all use some slowing down?

Fifth, Extremely strong...

The last thing that was spoken over Asher was that he was going to be strong and have strength. Those are the five blessings given to Asher by Moses. I believe that five is the number of grace, and I am going to ask God for all five blessings. I am going to ask him for my children to be blessed for the rest of their lives. I thank God that even though my family has rejected me, I am thankful to be accepted by God and His family; I ask that God have oil for my feet. No matter what sin I step into and no matter what I do, if I come back to Him, he will cleanse me, wash me, forgive me, and finally anoint me. Then I would like to put on some good brass. If you think about it, they used to wear those brass leggings when they went to war. Goliath had brass sheathes around his legs and they would just strap them in the back. Isn't it great that by studying His word we are armed with his two edged sword made of iron. Thank God, we have the armor of God found in Ephesians. That way no matter what happens, we will not fall, we're going to stay strong, and we are prepared for battle.

I want to show you a Scripture in Chronicles that pertains to the tribe of Asher, he blessed, anointed, accepted and strong.

1 Chronicles 7:40 *"All these were the children of Asher, heads of their father's house, choice and mighty men of valor, chief of the princes. And the number throughout the genealogy of them that were apt to war and to battle was twenty and six thousand men."*

The first thing I see in verse 40 is that they are choice and mighty men. They are men of valor. To call someone a 'man of valor' is a very high compliment. It means that you have character, morals, and your conduct brings no reproach on anybody. If you can visualize a man in uniform, you visualize his uniform being very crisp with pressed pleats, when I see someone who is well groomed and well dressed, I think to myself, here is a man of valor. Therefore, if you look at Scripture above, they are men who are leaders, choice men. The next thing I see in the Scripture is that they are men ready for battle. The children of Asher were ready for battle. Just try to imagine 26,000 men ready for battle. I have spoken about this previously, but no man is 'just' ready for battle. They have to go through boot camp and once they have gone through the war the after effects of battle can leave an individual undone.

One of the problems with the Vietnam War, compared to other wars, is that when they brought the men home from war they were never de-programmed. They never took them aside long enough to deal with all the emotional stress and damage and the effects of the war. It was drilled into these men to react mechanically, without even thinking. My husband was in Vietnam. He was a combat veteran of sixteen months. It has been over 40 years and still I have to let him know if I am going to make noise in the kitchen. If I do not tell him I am going to make some noise in the kitchen, he will over react. Even though my husband was ready for war, the war did alot to him. Do you know that for 30 years, he would never sit down at Christmas with us while our children opened presents? He would always stand. The kids would always ask him to sit with us while we open presents and he would always tell them he would be there in a minute. After some time he went for therapy with some other veterans and they asked him to talk about Christmas. Turns out, he was on high alert for two Christmases while he was in Vietnam. He had to lie in the grass from midnight until four, in the morning, listening for the enemy without falling asleep, while guarding the camp. I am telling you right now, I do not know if I could lie in the grass all alone in the dark of night, knowing an enemy is coming, for four to five hours just listening to the sounds of the night. I would be terrified. Here is what happened; as they began to talk to him, his whole life since he has been home has been on high alert. After a few weeks of therapy, we started to go back and look through our photographs. In each one, he always stood so that he could face the door, because subconsciously he was still on high alert. Here he was 30 years later, protecting his family. Now he sits down with us and he does not have to face the front door. We can open our presents and we do not have to worry about it. Once a man of valor has been trained for, war their training remains intact for life.

1 Chronicles 12:36 *"And of Asher, such as went forth to battle, expert in war, forty thousand."*

In this verse, we see that they were experts in war. You and I know that we are engaged in a battle. We have been enlisted whether we like it or not. I do not care if you are a peace lover and you do not want to fight. You have been enlisted. The minute we received Jesus; we left the kingdom of darkness, stepping into the kingdom of light, the war began to rage. The enemy wants to stop us from evangelizing and living a victorious Christian life. He will do anything to try to stop us. We had better get some of this spirit of the tribe of Asher in us. We need to say, you know what, 'I am a child of God, I am strong and I am anointed with oil, and I am going to wear brass, along with carrying a sword of iron as we put on the full armor of God.' I am not just going to be in a fight, I am going to be an expert in war. I am going to win. Who would fight to lose? I have only been in two fights and I have won them both.

Luke 2:36-38 *"And there was one Anna, a prophetess, the daughter of Phanuel, of the tribe of Asher: she was of a great age, and had lived with an husband seven years from her virginity; And she was a widow of about fourscore and four years, which departed not from the temple, but served God with fasting and prayers night and day. And she coming in that instant gave thanks likewise unto the Lord, and spake of him to all them that looked for redemption in Jerusalem."*

I want to shift gears a bit and show you a Scripture about a woman in the New Testament. This is awesome! Here is a woman in the temple when they are bringing Jesus in to dedicate him. There is an old man named Simeon who was there because the Holy Spirit led him there. He took one look at Jesus and said *"now I can depart and die in peace. I have seen the salvation of the Lord."* Anna comes in right at that moment and begins to preach Jesus to all the people in the synagogue and in Jerusalem. The first thing we see is her name, *Anna,* which means "grace" and that she is a prophetess. There are not a lot of women that are called prophetess. Just to name some of the women that were prophets in the Bible, they are:

> Miriam (Exodus 15:20)
> Deborah (Judges 4:4)
> Huldah (II Kings 22:14, II Chronicles 34:22)
> Noadiah (Nehemiah 6:14)
> The daughters of Philip (The book of Acts)
> Anna (Luke 2:36-68)

Anna was from the tribe of *Asher*, which means to be blessed and happy. Therefore, we see that Anna was a prophetess and she served God. In verse 37 it says that Anna was a widow. She departed not from the Temple, but she served God. Can you define the term to *serve* God? I think of service as doing something or helping someone. The root word for serve is 'to worship.' She worshipped. Do you know that worship is serving God? The twofold part of her ministry was that she fasted and prayed. What a statement to make about a woman, from the tribe of Asher. God wants you to know what tribe she came from, and that she belonged in the New Testament. She lived a life of valor and servant hood. She waited on God and worshiped him in the temple for 84 years or more, consecrated, living a life of fasting and prayer. Her reward was speaking of the Christ to all who were in the synagogue.

Four things to remember about Anna:

> 1. Prophetess
> 2. Served God
> 3. Fasted
> 4. Prayed

The color of the onyx stone is black. The Key Definition for onyx comes from the root word for onyx which means "nail." Now I can think of how black it was when Jesus was nailed to the cross because darkness prevailed over the land. There is something mentioned about the onyx stone in Genesis chapter 2 and it has something to do with manna. I told you earlier in this chapter that his bread would be fat and that he would have rich bread or rich food.

Genesis 2:12 *"And the gold of that land is good: there is bdellium and the onyx stone."*

The garden is good, the man is good, and everything is good. If you remember from the beginning of Genesis God is naming the four rivers. If you look at verse 10, it says that a river went out in all of Eden to water the garden and it becomes four heads of rivers. Then right after He named the rivers in verse 11. All I want you to know from this Scripture is that onyx is mentioned with the word bdellium and you only see that bdellium is only mentioned one more time in Scripture.

Numbers 11:6-7 *"But now our soul is dried away: there is nothing at all, beside this manna, before our eyes. And the manna was as coriander seed, and the color thereof as the color of bdellium."*

Now do not get confused and think that manna was black, because it was not. The word *bdellium* means "white, to be like a pearl." Why am I giving you these two unusual Scriptures about the onyx stone? So that you see the onyx was mentioned in the Garden of Eden and it was mentioned with this particular thing called a *bdellium*, which really represents manna, which is a white, pearl substance.

Do you know what the word *'manna'* means? The definition for *manna* is "what is it?" It was the bread of heaven. Jesus came years later and said that He was the manna, the Bread of Life, according to John 6. Manna tasted like a wafer with honey. I find it very interesting that the onyx stone would be mentioned in a verse that contains manna. Considering that Asher was promised to be blessed with bread, I think that if you and I can get bread from God, we have something to be very happy about.

The major point of this chapter is that you can get bread from God. If we can get fresh manna 'bread' from God and be fed, we should be happy. How much happier would our lives be if we could stay immersed in the manna in order to maintain a happy life.

The last thing I want to say about the onyx is that when the high priest would get ready to go into the presence of God, on both of his shoulders were large onyx stones. The names of the children of Israel were engraved on the onyx stones, six names on each stone according to their birth. Now, why are we looking at this?

Exodus 28:9-12 (NIV) *"Take two onyx stones and engrave on them the names of the sons of Israel in the order of their birth—six names on one stone and the remaining six on the other. Engrave the names of the sons of Israel on the two stones the way a gem cutter engraves a seal. Then mount the stones in gold filigree settings and fasten them on the shoulder pieces of the ephod as memorial stones for the sons of Israel. Aaron is to bear the names on his shoulders as a memorial before the LORD."*

The onyx stone carried the name of God's children as a memorial into God's presence. Just think with me for one moment. I want you to picture yourself at a very high elevation and we are all going to look down. Looking down from this high pinnacle, there is a man coming down the street. What is the very first thing you are going to see? You would clearly see his shoulders and the top of his head. It made me happy to realize that my name goes before the Lord and is one of the first things that He sees. My name is written in the Lamb's Book of Life as well as carried on His shoulders.

## Key Point

Simply put, Jesus is the bread of life, the message is to get bread from God and you will be happy.

## Closing Prayer

*Father, thank You for the Word. Like Asher, I want to be content and I want to be happy. If you would feed me, Lord, with bread that is convenient and make that bread fat, I know my soul will prosper and I will be happy. Lord, I thank You for this woman, Anna, from the tribe of Asher, who called herself blessed and happy. You know what Lord? I really am blessed and I am so happy to know that my name is written in the Lamb's Book of Life, just like You wrote the names of the sons of Israel on the shoulders of the priest. Lord, I thank You that You have done these won-*

*derful things for me. Father, as I am reminded that I have brass on my feet and a heavy iron sword in my hand, I just pray that I am equipped for war and that I am anointed with oil. I pray that I am strong, valiant and that I hold my head up high. I just want to thank You once again for Jesus Christ, because I am more than a conqueror through Him who loves me; in Jesus name, Amen.*

## CHAPTER 13

# – The Twelfth Stone –
# The Jasper of Naphtali

*Father, thank You for the Word of God, and we thank You that through this book, we are learning tremendous things. Lord, we do not want to get caught up with head knowledge. We want to gain heart knowledge and we want to let our light so shine before men that they would see our good works and glorify God. Thank You that we are living stones and that we are over Your heart just like the breastplate of the most high priest. Lord, as we look at this final stone, would You just touch our lives and help us to walk out this Christian life, bringing You glory and honor. In Jesus name, Amen.*

We are studying the last stone of the fourth row, which is the stone of jasper from the tribe of Naphtali. I will show you how the tribe of Naphtali was given its name. Looking back, we realize that Leah was one of the first of Jacob's wives to begin to name the twelve sons of Israel. Then after Leah had several sons, she gave one of her handmaidens to Jacob. Her handmaiden also had sons. Then Rachel had sons, and later Rachel's handmaiden gave birth to more sons.

Genesis 30:6-8 *"And Rachel said, God hath judged me, and hath also heard my voice, and hath given me a son: therefore she called his name Dan. Moreover, Bilhah, Rachel's maid, conceived again, and bare Jacob a second son. And Rachel said, with great wrestlings have I wrestled with my sister, and I have prevailed: and she called his name Naphtali"*

Recalling from chapter 11, *Dan's* name means "to judge." The Key Definition for *Naphtali* is "wrestlings." It is very sad how Rachel was full of envy and jealousy. She was so unhappy and wrestled with her own sister, at least in her own mind.

Ephesians 6:12 *"For we do not wrestle against flesh and blood, but against principalities, against powers, against the rulers of the darkness of this age, against spiritual hosts of wickedness in the heavenly places."*

The Bible makes it plain that we do not need to wrestle with each other. If I am wrestling against flesh and blood whom might our struggles be with? In studying the word 'wrestle' in Ephesians I was shocked to find out the definition was not the definition found in verse 8 of Genesis chapter 30. The word wrestle in Ephesians means to apply constant pressure, pinning the opponent, and never striking a blow. When the Bible talks about wrestling with the enemy, it is not like the men on television. You know the ones that I am talking about, where they wear the red suits and leap higher than a tall building, fly faster than a speeding bullet, and bang one another up for an hour leaving not a bruise. That is not what the book of Ephesians is talking about; it is a continual application of pressure upon your opponent, never striking a blow.

The definition for 'wrestlings' in Genesis chapter 30 verse 8 is 'strife and contention.' We have certainly covered this in chapters past. Rachel had a real problem. She named her son 'that I have struggled and wrestled until I prevailed over my sister.' There is nothing else to say except I think this is pitiful. When we get to the blessing of Moses, you will see that Naphtali has one of the most phenomenal blessings of all the twelve sons.

Before I show you his blessing, many of us have experienced contention or wrestlings in our walk with God. Sometimes I feel like Jacob. He wrestled all night and said, 'I'm not going to let you go until you bless me.' Therefore, the angel of the Lord puts Jacob's hip out of joint, and he walks with a limp for the rest of his life. He can say that God blessed him and he knows what it is to struggle with God and with human nature.

In the Old Testament, before the men of old or patriarchs prepared to die, they would call all of their children around them so that they could speak blessings upon them. Afterwards they would give up the ghost. I do not know about you, but I would really like the Lord to tell me when my time is over. I would like to bring my family around me and speak blessings over them before I depart.

I do not know how many of you have ever heard of the late John Osteen. His son, Joel Osteen, has that awesome church in Lakewood. When Joel's father John was dying, he knew it, and he called his family in and began to speak blessings over each one. When he pronounced blessings over his wife Dodie (Dolores) and each one of his sons, they began to wash his feet. In the end, his children spoke into his life through this act of servant hood, declaring what a great man of God he was. When his wife Dodie washed his feet, John closed his eyes and went to be with the Lord. She was the last one to see him alive. What a way to go, when you think of it, according to the Bible.

Genesis 49:21 *"Naphtali is a hind let loose: he giveth goodly words."*

This verse did not make any sense to me as it says that he was a "hind let loose." It is an awesome thing when God lets us loose of our wrestlings or struggles. I can look back at the struggle and wrestlings and see that they weren't a struggle at all for God. Because I let loose of it, God was glorified. God wants to free us from anything that we wrestle with. Whenever an animal is in captivity and are set loose, it is such great victory. Then the second part of the verse goes on to say that he speaks goodly words.

James 3:8 *"But the tongue can no man tame; [it is] an unruly evil, full of deadly poison."*

I wanted to remind us of how important our words are. He speaks good and kind words. I do not know if I ever really understood that the words that we speak are literally creative. You know how God said, 'let there be... and there was?' I am not God, so I never really connected with the fact that our words can actually create. A friend of mine mentioned that if I say certain things to you, I could create anger in you. Isn't that the truth? If I say kind words to you, I can create warmth inside of you. How true it is that our words really do affect people. I do not know about you, but if someone says a harsh or critical word to me, that stays with me longer than I would like. It is like indelible ink and it feels like it has been tattooed in your mind. If someone gets critical of you it stays with you. You can relive those words at any time. However, when you get compliments and praise, it rolls off of you. Why is it that our words wound? Because the tongue is so hard to tame. Even from the book of James we know that we can tame all sorts of animals but the tongue no man can tame.

One of my husband's favorite scriptures is found in the book of Matthew.

Matthew 12:33-37 *"Either make the tree good, and his fruit good; or else make the tree corrupt, and his fruit corrupt: for the tree is known by his fruit. O generation of vipers, how can ye, being evil, speak good things? For out of the abundance of the heart the mouth speaketh. A good man out of the good treasure of the heart bringeth forth good things: and an evil man out of the evil treasure bringeth forth evil things. But I say unto you, That every idle word that men shall speak, they shall give account thereof in the day of judgment. For by thy words thou shalt be justified, and by thy words thou shalt be condemned."*

So, if indeed we are looking at Naphtali speaking goodly words, then how important are our words? We are going to have to give an account, so we should continually remember to ask the Lord to forgive us for speaking the idle words. It is difficult to go back and try to remember all the things that we say. Since I can't remember all the wasted words I have spoken, it seems to me the best thing to do is to repent. Do not even try to figure it out. Just say, "Lord, I'm sorry for speaking wasteful, idle words. Let me produce good words out of the good fruit in my heart."

Deuteronomy 33:23 *"And of Naphtali he said, O Naphtali, satisfied with favor, and full with the blessing of the LORD: possess thou the west and the south."*

There are three parts to this verse. The first blessing is that Naphtali will be satisfied with favor. The second blessing is that he is full of the blessing of the Lord. I am going to try to remember this when I get into my next wrestling match. With God's help, I can have favor and be full of blessings. The third blessing is that he possesses the West and South. I want to break this down and take a look at the favor that he has, the blessings that we have, and what it means to possess the West and South.

Psalm 5:12 *"For thou, LORD, wilt bless the righteous; with favor wilt thou compass him as with a shield."*

This Psalm speaks about God's favor being *a shield around about us,* and that His favor will compass around us. *Compass* means, "encircle or to surround or enclose with a shield." We see in this passage of Scripture that favor is a shield. Back in Deuteronomy, it speaks of Naphtali being satisfied with favor. In this particular Scripture *favor* is defined as, "to be accepted and to have good will." Therefore, God accepts us and wants to do His good will in our lives. Isn't acceptance the very thing everyone wants? I do not care if you are young or old; everybody wants someone in their life to accept them. You know, just to be accepted for who you are.

This is the cry of every teenager. To be accepted for who they are. Every teenager, when they get to that awkward age, struggles with acceptance. Since they are not considered an adult, yet, they do not consider themselves a child, they feel like they are in limbo. Where do I fit in? I am not a child nor am I an adult. I just want to be accepted. So that is what the word favor means. It means that God accepts you just as you are. Once He has accepted us, His favor surrounds us like a shield.

Look at what a shield was in the day of the Bible. In the movies, we usually see the diamond shape shield or a round shield. In the Bible when these men of Israel made a shield it actually covered the top of their heads and went down to their feet. It had a roof and it went all the way to the ground so that when the enemy would shoot fiery arrows, they would hide under their shield for protection. The arrows would hit the top of the shield. The only thing that would be exposed would be their back and that's why they had each other. Understand that the favor of God is a shield all about us. It covers us completely, on every side, so that when the enemy shoots his fiery arrows we are totally protected. You just have to walk around and say, "Hey, wait a minute, I have the favor of God with me and God has accepted me." It may be difficult to walk around and proclaim that you are one of God's favorites, but that is the Word of God making it truth. If we continue to confess it and declare that we are God's favorites, then we might even begin to believe it and possess it. I will tell you one thing, I am convinced that I am one of God's favorites and so are you. He has shielded me round about, over-the-top, and in every direction with His favor, which means He has accepted me.

We think that we have to do something to get favor, like I have to be good to you and then down the road, you will return the favor and be good to me. God's favor is completely one-sided; there is nothing I could give God to earn His favor. It is a gift that He accepts us just as we are. Therefore, Naphtali is satisfied with favor. If you look at your life for a minute, would you be able to say that you are satisfied with favor? I ask this because there are some areas in my life where I am not satisfied. I was wondering, "Lord how do I become satisfied with favor?" I need to be satisfied in just knowing that You accccept me. You want to add blessings to my life and You are shielding me with favor. Like the Apostle Paul, I want to learn to be content in all things. The secret is to be content and satisfied in all things.

> Isaiah 49:8 *"Thus saith the LORD, In an acceptable time have I heard thee, and in a day of salvation have I helped thee: and I will preserve thee, and give thee for a covenant of the people, to establish the earth, to cause to inherit the desolate heritages;"*

Now the Scripture actually reads better in the NIV. However, I wanted to prove the point that the word favor means acceptance by reading it in the KJV. Here is what I want to show you: *"in an acceptable time, I have heard thee,"* the word *acceptable* in the Hebrew is defined as "favor." Therefore, in other words, it literally means in the day of my favor, I have heard you and will help you.

The second thing about Naphtali, I want to show you is that he is full of blessings as seen back in Deuteronomy. I thought the word blessing would be defined as expectancy; maybe something good was going to happen such as protection or prosperity. I was so surprised to find out what it really meant when I looked it up. In the book of Deuteronomy, the Key Definition for *blessing* is, "a gift that brings peace." As a matter of fact, the word *blessing* is a treaty of peace. You want to know what it is to have the blessings of God. It means that you have peace no matter what is happening. Look around this world, people are struggling to have peace. With the weather, our culture, the economy, and job loss, many of us have lost our peace. I thought to myself, the blessing of the Lord brings us a treaty of peace. Obviously, I do not know much about treaties. However, a treaty may also be known as an agreement, protocol, covenant, convention, and exchange of letters between two parties. God will never break His promises and His word is the letter of agreement with us. Therefore, the word *'bless-*

*ing*' means to 'receive a treaty of peace.'

Isaiah 32:17-18 *"And the work of righteousness shall be peace; and the effect of righteousness quietness and assurance forever. And my people shall dwell in a peaceable habitation, and in sure dwellings, and in quiet resting places."*

I used to put the Scripture from this verse on postcards and would quote it to my children, "I have a house of peace, now knock it off!" Whether or not you can relate to that, one thing I am sure of is that we have a treaty of peace. Naphtali not only had favor from God, but he had peace; even though his mother named him, 'to wrestle and to struggle.' Just think what we could accomplish if we did not lose our peace. No matter what we wrestle with, no matter what our struggle is, we have God's favor. If we will hold on to it, we don't have to lose our peace.

Isaiah 26:3 *"Thou wilt keep him in perfect peace, whose mind is stayed on thee: because he trusteth in thee."*

Here is our problem, we think about everything except keeping our mind fixed and focused on God. We let our minds wander and run; in turn getting us all worked up. The next thing you know, we have indigestion, we can't sleep at night and the anti-depressant business is through the roof. The Bible says 'we can have perfect peace if our minds stay on Him.' And just remember this, no matter what you wrestle with, God has accepted you. Even if you fail the test or fall short, God accepts you. He is not going to get rid of you and he is not going to reject you. People will accept you if you do what they want, or if you please them, but God accepts us just the way we are.

Ephesians 1:1-3 *"Paul, an apostle of Jesus Christ by the will of God, to the saints which are at Ephesus, and to the faithful in Christ Jesus: Grace be to you, and peace, from God our Father, and from the Lord Jesus Christ. Blessed be the God and Father of our Lord Jesus Christ, who hath blessed us with all spiritual blessings in heavenly places in Christ:"*

Who hath blessed us; what tense is 'hath blessed' us? It is past tense; therefore we have already been blessed. We're not going to be blessed, we are already blessed. What we have to realize is that we have to agree with the word because we are already blessed with all spiritual blessings in heavenly places in Christ. We are blessed far above all powers and principalities. The Bible says we are 'blessed going in and blessed coming out.' A friend of mine had a T-shirt that said, "I am too blessed to be stressed." She used to wear it all the time and you know, I never saw her stressed or uptight. How do you think we get this blessing? I think that prayer and obedience bring blessings to us; whatever you can do to obey God brings a blessing. Spending time in His presence brings us more spiritual blessings.

Meditate on theses verse and then recite this: "I am and have been blessed with all spiritual blessings in heavenly places in Christ Jesus." Now all we have to do is to keep our minds in heavenly places.

This is the next question that I have: why, out of all the tribes and all of the stones that we have studied, does not one of them talk about direction as far as possessing North, South, East or West? Most of us, if we were going to give directions, would say go right, left, down the street, or up the street; we would normally not give directional headings such as; North, South, East and West. We would not talk like this and say we are going to go West and South. So, why is it that Naphtali gets to possess the West and South?

I selected two Scripture verses to review with you in regards to the West and the South. Several years ago, I was reading the book of Ezekiel chapter 37 where it talks about the valley of dry bones. If you know the story, the prophet says that God put him in the middle of the valley of dry bones, God told him to prophesy or to speak. So he prophesied and there was a noise and behold a shaking and the bones came together, bone to bone. The 'sinews and the flesh came up upon them and the skin covered them above, but there was no breath.' When I was a kid, my father used to love the song, *Them Bones, Them Bones,* and we used to go around the house singing, "the ankle bone's connected to the..." At the end of the verse we would all sing together "..hear the word of the Lord." My father just loved that song and it was not until years later that I even saw this story in the Bible. Back before iPods and computers, we used to have 78 speed records. You would pick up the arm of the record player, put the needle on the record and listen to the song. One day I was reading that story and I noticed something that I hadn't noticed before.

Ezekiel 37:9 *"Then said he unto me, Prophesy unto the wind, prophesy, son of man, and say to the wind, Thus saith the Lord GOD; Come from the four winds, O breath, and breathe upon these slain, that they may live."*

Even though the bones came together and there was a shaking, there was no life in the bones until the prophet called the four winds. There are four directions or four winds that the Bible talks about: 'North, South, East, and West.' The *North* is 'a place of cleansing.' In the book of Job, it says that 'the North wind cleansed me and passed through me.' So the North wind is a wind of cleansing that has to go through you. After the North, we have the *South* wind, which is 'a place of renewal and refreshing.' When the Word of God calls for the North wind as a wind of cleansing, He then calls for the South wind, as a wind of renewal and refreshing. Now the East wind is a wind that I really do not want to deal with because the *East* wind is 'our wind of correction.' From the East, God corrects.

The *West* wind 'reverses the curse.' In Exodus chapter 10 verse 19 you see that the West wind comes to drive all of the locusts out of the land. What I really find interesting is what the word West means in this particular verse. The word West is defined as 'roar.' How many times have we had the Lord roar into our lives and reverse something that we had no control over? In a minute, God blows his breath to resolve it. To have the West wind blow over your life or to possess the West is awesome because it reverses the curse. Catch this; the *North* wind is 'a wind of cleansing,' the *South* wind is 'a place of refreshing and renewal,' the *East* wind is 'the wind of correction' and the *West* wind 'reverses the curse.'

So what does Naphtali possess? He's not only satisfied with favor, accepted, and full of blessings; which is a gift of the treaty of peace; but then he possesses the West. As struggles come into your life, try to live as Naphtali did looking to the West where the curse has been reversed, and then let the winds from South refresh and renew your spirit. So to finish his story, when the Prophet called for the four winds from the North, South, East and West the dry bones began to stand up and became an Army for God.

Isaiah 59:19 *"So shall they fear the name of the LORD from the west, and his glory from the rising of the sun. When the enemy shall come in like a flood, the Spirit of the LORD shall lift up a standard against him."*

If we will have a fear of the Lord, it says that those who fear the Lord come from the West. I am convinced that if we fear and reverence God, he will reverse curses in our lives and that he will keep the enemy at bay and far from us. I personally think that if you fear Him from the West, God will raise up a standard. I have heard this verse so many times and heard it taught so many different ways, but I have never heard anyone speak of fearing the name of the Lord from the West. Now I want to give you something to think about. There are two ways to look at this familiar Scripture, and I believe they both are correct. I believe that they both can happen at different seasons of your life. The way I usually hear people quote this verse is, "When the enemy comes in like a flood, the Spirit of the Lord shall lift up a standard." Keep in mind that every comma, period, capital letter and semi-colon in your Bible was put there by man. I hope you know that the Bible was written in all upper case letters, they didn't have chapters, didn't have book divisions or any of the distinctions that we have in our Bibles today. Commentators took a verse and put their inflection where they thought it should go. They decided to put a comma here and a semi-colon there. After hearing that Scripture quoted many times, the Spirit of the Lord spoke to me and asked, "Who in the Bible is represented by the flood?" If you go through all of the Scriptures in the Bible that speak of water or floods, it talks of God. There are a couple Scriptures that talk about water and the enemy, but there are very few. Here is how the Lord spoke this Scripture to me: 'when the enemy comes in, like a flood, the Spirit of the Lord shall lift up a standard against him.' So, you can have one from column A, or one from column B, it is your choice. There have been times in my life when the enemy has come in like a flood, and there have been other times where before the enemy even comes in God raises a flood against him and drowns out all his plans against me. You very rarely hear the beginning of this promise quoted where we have fear of the Lord from the West.

Seal this statement into your spirit by reading this several times.

"I am like Naphtali: satisfied with favor, full of blessings, possessing the West and the South"

Now remember, the West represents those who fear God, and he will lift up a standard.

Psalm 78:25-26 *"Man did eat angels' food: he sent them meat to the full. He caused an east wind to blow in the heaven: and by his power he brought in the south wind."*

The reason I wanted to go over this Scripture about Naphtali possessing the West and South is what the South means in this verse; and it does not mean Florida! The word South in this verse means, 'authority at the right hand' and we know who that is... Jesus! When you possess the South, it means that you know Him who is ever present at the right hand of God. I think of all the tribes that we have been over; and I'll take the one in Deuteronomy chapter 33 verse 23 any day.

The color of the jasper stone is translucent and it resembles the color of fire. It is a mixture of blazing reds, oranges, and yellows, the same color as fire. We are going to look at three Scriptures about the jasper stone found in the book of Revelation. How appropriate it is to have this as the last stone. We are going to end all of this with favor and blessing, fear of the Lord and Jesus at the right hand.

Revelation 4:1-3 *"After this I looked, and behold, a door was opened in heaven: and the first voice which I heard was as it were of a trumpet talking with me; which said, Come up hither, and I will shew thee things which must be hereafter. And immediately I was in the spirit: and, behold, a throne was set in heaven, and one sat on the throne. And he that sat was to look upon like a jasper and a sardine stone: and there was a rainbow round about the throne, in sight like unto an emerald."*

Revelation 21:10-11 *"And he carried me away in the spirit to a great and high mountain, and showed me that great city, the holy Jerusalem, descending out of heaven from God, Having the glory of God: and her light was like unto a stone most precious, even like a jasper stone, clear as crystal;"*

Revelation 21: 18-19 *"And the building of the wall of it was of jasper: and the city was pure gold, like unto clear glass. And the foundations of the wall of the city were garnished with all manner of precious stones. The first foundation was jasper; the second, sapphire; the third, a chalcedony; the fourth, an emerald;"*

Revelation speaks that the jasper is God's appearance. Remember, our

God is an all-consuming fire and the jasper stone represents the presence and the glory of God. It says, 'when I looked at Him, His appearance was like a jasper stone, like fire.'

## Key Points

I am going to walk around declaring the following; 'I am full of favor and full of blessings, coming in and going out, because I possess the West as I fear God, and He has reversed the curse in my life and raises up a standard against the enemy. I possess the South, where Jesus is positioned at the right hand of God on my behalf. You know that we cannot retain all this just because it has been written and read. God's glory, God's appearance and God's foundation for us is favor and blessing. How appropriate in this study that the last stone represents the glory of God, the appearance of God, and being full of favor and blessing. It is my hope that the truth written within this book will seep into our hearts.

## Closing Prayer

*Father, I thank You that I am favored of God. Help me to keep this mindset. Lord, I thank You that You have accepted me and that as You said about Naphtali, I am also satisfied with favor, full of blessing and have been given the treaty of peace. I thank You that I possess the West and South. I thank You, because those that fear the Lord from the West know that when the enemy comes in, then like a flood You raise up a standard against him. I thank You that the South is a place of renewal and refreshing at the right hand of God. Lord, as I reflect upon the jasper stone, it is a clear stone that represents flames of fire, like You who is an All Consuming Fire, that causes me to draw near to the flame. Help me Lord, in my struggles and through the challenges of my life. I know that the glory of God is upon me, and the glory of God is within me. And Lord, now that I have studied these stones, I can get a glimpse of what it will someday be like to see the City of God with all of the precious stones; it will be magnificent. I thank you that the foundation of the Holy City is the jasper stone; everything is built upon the Glory of God. I long for You to be glorified in my life and I know that You satisfy me with favor. Thank You that I am full of blessing, that I possess the fear of God and that from the South, Your power has brought Jesus to the right hand of God.*

*I thank You for each and every stone in the breastplate. May I be as a living stone and a royal priesthood, to the Glory of God, in Jesus Name, Amen.*

# CHAPTER 14

## — Charts and Tables —

*Key Point Table*

| | The Sardius: Judah | The Topaz: Issachar | The Carbuncle: Zebulun |
|---|---|---|---|
| **Row 1** | Because of the Blood of Jesus we can give praise to God | You are rewarded for service | We dwell in the light |
| | **The Emerald: Reuben** | **The Sapphire: Simeon** | **The Diamond: Gad** |
| **Row 2** | Throne of the First Born will see Jesus, this is the Covenant of Promise | God has heard me and is polishing me through affliction | We are more than conquerors through the crown of Jesus, the Great Lion who bruised Satan |
| | **The Ligure: Ephraim** | **The Agate: Manasseh** | **The Amethys: Benjamin** |
| **Row 3** | Doubly fruitful in affliction yields a double portion of joy | Causing me to forget the pain of my past and pressing on toward the high calling | Jesus is seated at the right hand of the Father and one day will welcome me |
| | **The Beryl: Dan** | **The Onyx: Asher** | **The Jasper: Naphtali** |
| **Row 4** | Subdue the serpent by making a right judgment | Causing me to be happy because I have the Bread of Heaven | I am satisfied with favor and full of blessings |

# Jacob, His Four Wives, 12 Sons and Daughter

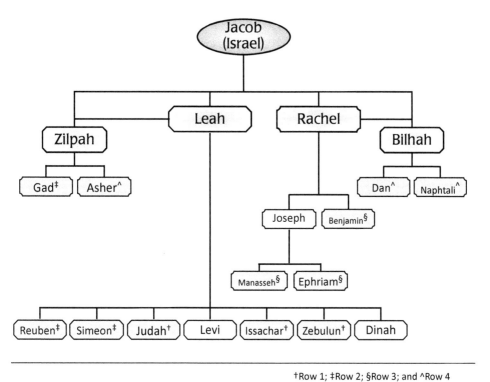

†Row 1; ‡Row 2; §Row 3; and ^Row 4

Handmaiden

Twelve Tribes

Omitted from breastplate

*Key Definition (Alphabetical) Table*

| Name | Key Definition |
|------|----------------|
| Agate | Streams of flames |
| Amethyst | To dream |
| Asher | To be blessed and happy |
| Benjamin | Son at my right hand or son of my right hand |
| Benoni | Son of my sorrow |
| Bilhah | To be troubled |
| Blessing | A gift that brings peace |
| Carbuncle | Glittering or brilliant lights |
| Dan | Judge, or to pass a judgment |
| Diamond | To break in pieces by bruising |
| Ephraim | Fruitful in affliction |
| Gad | Fortunate |
| Issachar | To be rewarded |
| Jacob | A trickster or a deceiver |
| Joseph | To add on or add to |
| Judah | Praise be unto God |
| Leah | Weary, out of strength |
| Ligure | To engrave a seal |
| Manasseh | Helping me to forget the past |
| Naphtali | To struggle or to wrestle |
| Nazarite | Consecrated, to be devoted to God |
| Rachel | A ewe, a female sheep |
| Reuben | Behold a firstborn son |
| Sapphire | Polishing or to be polished |
| Sardius | Red, carnelian (redness) |
| Simeon | God heard me in my affliction |
| Zebulun | To dwell with honor |
| Zephath | Watchtower |
| Zilpah | Trickling, a very slow flowing river |

*The Exhaustive Dictionary of Bible Names,* Dr. Judson Cornwall and Dr. Stelman Smith, Bridge-Logos Publishers

*Hebrew-Greek Key Study Bible* (See Old Testament Lexical Aids), AMG Publishers

*Strong's Exhaustive Concordance of the Bible,* Thomas Nelson Publisher

Blue Letter Bible, http://www.blueletterbible.org

# Additional books by Gwen Mouliert

## Satan's Secret Weapon

*— The Bite of Bitterness —*

### *Destroy Satan's Secret Weapon — Pain and Bitterness! —*

Satan wants to keep these secrets hidden from you! The enemy is looking to establish roots of bitterness in every Christian. Don't let even tiny seeds of pain or bitterness grow into a stronghold. In this exciting book, you'll learn how to identify and destroy the venom of the viper.

You can escape from Satan's trap! Experience tremendous peace, happiness, and joy in your soul. Find new freedom! Don't let Satan deceive you. Examine key Scriptures and safeguard your heart from other people's rebellion and deceit. Renew your faith in God's ability to heal. Learn how to swing the ax of forgiveness! You'll never want to face Satan's secret weapon again! Protect yourself from all roots of bitterness. Don't give Satan any opportunity to steal from you!!! Every Christian needs God's cure for the seeds of bitterness that Satan tries to plant.

---

## Hyper to Holiness

*— How Jesus Touched the Life of a Housewife —*

From humble beginnings to an international ministry; in this autobiography, Gwen shares her joys and sorrows in honesty and truth. Her deep personal relationship with the Lord reflected in the pages of this book. You will discover how the daily application of God's Word can produce great and mighty things in your life and come to realize what Jesus can do for you!

*Revised edition available 2011*

---

Proclaiming His Word | PO Box 941 | Pomona, NJ 08240 | (609) 407-1753 |
info@proclaiminghisword.org | www.proclaiminghisword.org

CPSIA information can be obtained
at www.ICGtesting.com
Printed in the USA
BVHW052159220623
666253BV00016B/981

9 780615 363066